WE TAKE OUR CITIES WITH US

MACHETE
Joy Castro, Series Editor

WE TAKE OUR CITIES WITH US

A Memoir

SORAYYA KHAN

MAD CREEK BOOKS, AN IMPRINT OF
THE OHIO STATE UNIVERSITY PRESS
COLUMBUS

Published by Mad Creek Books, an imprint of The Ohio State University Press.

Library of Congress Cataloging-in-Publication Data

Names: Khan, Sorayya, author.

Title: We take our cities with us : a memoir / Sorayya Khan.

Other titles: Machete.

Description: Columbus : Mad Creek Books, an imprint of The Ohio State University Press, [2022] | Series: Machete | Summary: "A Pakistani-Dutch writer's multicultural memoir of grief and immigrant experience that illuminates the complexities of identity and inheritance in a global world"—Provided by publisher.

Identifiers: LCCN 2022018754 | ISBN 9780814258484 (paperback) | ISBN 0814258484 (paperback) | ISBN 9780814282403 (ebook) | ISBN 0814282407 (ebook)

Subjects: LCSH: Khan, Sorayya. | Novelists, American—21st century—Biography.

Classification: LCC PS3611.H35 Z46 2022 | DDC 818/.603 [B]—dc23/eng/20220623

LC record available at https://lccn.loc.gov/2022018754

Cover design by adam bohannon

Text design by Juliet Williams

Type set in Adobe Garamond Pro

♾ The paper used in this publication meets the minimum requirements of the American National Standard for Information Sciences—Permanence of Paper for Printed Library Materials. ANSI Z39.48-1992.

ALSO BY SORAYYA KHAN

City of Spies
Five Queen's Road
Noor

For you—
my mother, Thera,
and your mother, Eleonora.

MY MOTHER, THERA, AND ME, IN LAHORE, PAKISTAN, JANUARY 1963.

ONE

My mother was white and my father was brown, my mother Dutch, my father Pakistani. If she'd had a choice, she would have been brown. She tried, sitting near swimming pools during short summers when we lived in Vienna and long ones when we lived in Islamabad, but her attempts came to a full stop with basal cell carcinoma, when sunscreen replaced sun as her best friend. My father's brown was constant, except that when he grew older and gray, in a certain light and on a certain part of him, his color lightened. I am in between. I pretend I didn't know I was brown until we moved from Austria to Pakistan and I saw it all around and made it mine. But my truth of color and country is complicated.

Color is a fact for my American-born children. We didn't wake up one morning and decide our children were ready for the news: *You're brown.* Almost as soon as they could talk, they put their little arms next to mine and decided they were darker. They were always right, because when summer came and my color deepened, so did theirs and our skin tone never matched. Next to their father's, their arms and legs were not a match, but close enough.

"That's okay," our sons said about my outsider status and patted my arm because they must have thought I needed comforting.

Before long, they asked, "Where are we from?"

I'd say, "You are from where we are from, Pakistan. And from where you were born, here."

Naeem, my husband, would remember my mother and add, "Also from Holland, where Nani is from," which would surprise me because I had forgotten.

There is no flag for their combination and, anyway, the white in that equation, the one-fourth of them that is my mother, was ignored even then. "Nani is the brownest person we know," I heard them say once, as if they'd always known that color was a state of mind, not pigment.

My mother's allegiance to brown was resolute. She was forever on the side of the underdog, as if she'd lived it coming of age in Amsterdam during World War II as the daughter, granddaughter, and great-granddaughter of white Catholics. She'd half-joke, "I'm ab-so-lute-ly positive I have Arab blood in me," and then react to our skepticism with, "Now, don't you forget about the Arabs in Spain or the war between the Dutch and Spanish!" She threw around history the way all of us had been thrown around the world.

I knew then that history lived alongside us, but until she was gone, I didn't understand that her history lived there as well. She was right, you cannot leave history behind. But when you are the daughter of my mother, Thera, you cannot leave her behind either.

•

It's true, that day was warm and beautiful in New York. Summer bled into fall, trees were gloriously green, the sky more Colorado than New York, the freshly washed school buses a striking yellow. The scene never lasts long in Ithaca, where trees shed leaves before we'd like and snow arrives with Halloween. I walked to the afternoon bus stop with my neighbor, as I did most days since moving to the street. She'd seen her older child through elementary school, while I was still new to the routine. Shahid had started kindergarten the previous Thursday, without a backward glance as his little body climbed the bus steps behind Kamal, who was beginning fourth grade. The doors closed, the brakes released, and my relief was immediate: time had moved back into my life, more precious than when parenting stole it, and I was free.

We'd heard the news, of course. At first, the blaring radio in a repairman's white van on the side of the street was only a disruption. Sitting at my desk facing the window I'd slammed closed, I was desperate not to squander a moment of work time. I turned up the volume on Nusrat Fateh Ali Khan's *Devotional Songs* CD in my computer and checked email through our dial-up modem. As soon as I disconnected, the telephone rang and a friend gave me the news. By the time the phone calls stopped, the towers had fallen and Muslims were suspects.

Charlotte,* a neighbor, was reserved at the best of times, but at the bus stop that afternoon, so was I. "It's such a beautiful day," she finally said. "Here, at least," I responded, my single nod to the morning's events, to which she didn't reply. I knew better than to say more. The metrics lay between us, the way facts sometimes take up space. She, white. Me, brown. Me, Muslim. She, Jewish. Worst of all, I imagine, me, Pakistani.

The boys stumbled off the bus, careening into me like they still did in those days, Shahid running into my legs, Kamal close behind but measured in his steps. As we walked home, the boys' chatter filled the air. In the laundry room, the children threw down their backpacks and took off their shoes, and I said I had something important to tell them. Moments later, I leaned back against the kitchen sink, the edge of it in my lower back, the two of them looking up at me, smaller than usual. I said that two

---

* Some names and identifying characteristics have been changed. The stories and dialogue in this book are true to the best of the author's memory, and in respect to events the author was not present for, she has done her best to recreate them as they were told to her and with available information.

airplanes had flown into two tall buildings in New York City, the buildings had come crashing down, and thousands of people were dead. The planes were likely piloted by Muslims, I added. When their faces were still blank, I wondered if the moment would define their young lives the way the hanging of Prime Minister Zulfikar Ali Bhutto had defined mine.

"By accident, Mama?" Kamal asked.

"Why?" Shahid wondered.

A while later, their lunchboxes clattered on the counter and water splashed in the sink as they fought to be first to wash their hands. Snacks were on the table, perhaps ants on a log—a recent trick of peanut butter, celery, and raisins learned from a friend. Eventually, I turned on the radio and set the volume low, as Kamal bowed his head to math worksheets and Shahid to Harry Potter. That was their world at ages nine and five, as ours changed.

Before the week was out, a boy his age told Kamal on the bus that he would come to our house and kill us all. He'd been Kamal's second-grade classmate when he bragged about owning a shotgun, a detail we'd once discussed over dinner. I knew his father, as much as I could know a man who dressed in fatigues on Tuesday afternoons and said nothing while we waited by the classroom door to take our children to after-school activities. The boy's name was Gunner, not yet irony, merely fact, like the blond crop of unruly hair which fell over his eyes. The same day, also on the bus, another child called Shahid a terrorist. Our kindergartener understood the import, but not the word.

"What's a terrorist?" he asked at bedtime.

"Someone who causes terror," I responded.

"What's a terrorist?" he insisted, dissatisfied with my answer.

"It depends on which side of a fight you're on," Naeem explained because *terrorist* is complicated when you're a political science college professor speaking to a five-year-old who is your son, has been to Pakistan, and like all five-year-olds, understands a thing or two about justice.

More than the boys' faces or what was said, I remember the window above the front door. After, when they were asleep and we were not, I stood and faced it at the top of the stairs. Behind me was a Pakistani painting, all red and orange, that my mother called *The Storm*. On a rare winter day, sunlight floods the stairs and transforms them into a perfect place to read. At that time of night, rather than mirrored reflections of the painting or evidence of the porch light outside, the window framed a perfect square of black. Naeem turned off a living room lamp and the window leaned into the room, angles amiss, as if it too had moved.

"Be careful," my mother said when we spoke, although I hadn't told her what had happened with the boys. It was the middle of the night for me, morning in Vienna, and I'd called.

"I *am* careful," I replied, annoyed at the suggestion that I wasn't.

"The world has changed, my darling," she said.

"What do you think will happen?"

"War, of course," she said. "It's always war."

She was right, except it felt like it had already started.

A week or two later in September, during the school's open house for parents, Shahid's kindergarten teacher began by sharing that she'd fled the classroom when the news arrived. Miss Simon had family who were first responders and needed to know if they were alive. They were, she assured us, and we all breathed deeply and agreed that it had been a tough few weeks. Like Shahid, that year was Miss Simon's first in school, the beginning of her teaching career. She led us through our children's days, lingering over the school's new math curriculum and community building on the corner rug. As an aside, she described hand hugs, her quick double squeeze while she held hands with a child who needed extra comfort—walking him to the nurse or back from lunch or any time at all. Miss Simon was young and lovely, full of life as only someone who is passionate about her work can be. Not long after the evening, we were informed that Shahid used an art lesson to sketch two tall buildings, a worry for Miss Simon and the school administration. We were shown the dog-eared picture, a crude crayon drawing of a skyline on recycled paper, but we were not permitted to leave with it. We could only guess at the worry behind the blue drawing. He'd alluded to something we should have kept from him? Did the buildings, still standing in his rendering, suggest support for the pilots? What had we missed in the drawing? When asked, Shahid couldn't remember it, and without being able to produce it for him, it stayed that way.

One afternoon on the school bus, with no better grasp of the term, Shahid was again called a terrorist, and this time Rich told him he was going to kill him. "Only Gunner has guns, right?" Shahid asked when he got off the bus.

Right away, I telephoned the principal who promised to take care of the matter. Trusting that he had, we put Shahid on the bus the next morning, but on the afternoon ride it happened again. We met with the principal who said he'd dropped the ball. Despite the sports analogy, the Americanism never failed to irritate me, as if it should be possible to make things right by locating a dropped ball, picking it up, and putting it in its place. Shahid leaned in to me out of habit, almost but not quite on my lap. The principal praised us for our calm. He confided that the parent of another child on the same bus had stormed into his office the day his son was called a terrorist. The child was Black, and although Christian, his name was mistaken for Muslim. "Either you take care of this, or I will," the parent had said, and the spectacle of an imposing foreigner issuing an angry ultimatum had us uncomfortably smiling in sympathy.

Before the meeting ended, the principal asked Shahid, "How do you feel?"

He slowly pulled away from me, until he was standing on his own. "Fine," he smiled, sweeping his long-lashed gaze at us all. As we left, Shahid put his hand in mine and squeezed it twice.

•

My children don't believe me when I tell them there was a time Pakistan wasn't known to everyone I met. I struggled with this, more than anything, when I arrived at a small college in western Pennsylvania in 1979. It was worse, even, than *alien* written in the corner of my work-study pay checks. When students asked where I was from, Pakistan—beside Pittsburgh or Pottstown or Philadelphia—meant little except that I was foreign. One morning early along, Nick, a fellow freshman, fell into step with me while walking to the post office. He asked me where I was from and when I gave him Pakistan, he was excited and replied, "I know where that is! Next to Egypt!" Egypt's Anwar Sadat and the Camp David Peace Accords were in the news, which made me feel like he'd tried, and I couldn't bring myself to correct him. Every so often, someone asked a flurry of questions, like when the local post office called the dormitory payphone to deliver a telegram from home and the person who transcribed the message on the whiteboard on my door asked questions she'd already asked, as if my answers might have changed.

"What do they speak there?"

"Are there roads there?"

"Do you ride camels to school?"

And, always, "Where's your accent?" for which there was never an easy answer, although it made me feel as if I ought to be able to pull it from my pocket or quote a specific location where I'd left it behind.

"My language is yours," I'd finally say, which wasn't an answer and sounded wrong, but I stuck with it anyway.

I met Dawn during the first or second week of college at our work-study jobs. Dawn was Black and from Cleveland, and she embraced me as family the first time we spoke. Her single mother raised three daughters, and when I sat across from her at Thanksgiving one year, and then again and again, she beamed her love at me with a permanent grin and sparkling eyes. "Come on, baby, eat something." At her mother's home, I learned bacon came in turkey and baby wasn't just for babies and you could say, "Now, I know you're not talking to me," to your boyfriend when you were in the kitchen making dinner and he was sitting on the living room windowsill saying something you didn't like. Dawn and I went to her grandmother's house so she could do her grandmother's hair. With a standing lamp spread like silver tree limbs in a corner, Dawn set white hair in curlers while her grandmother asked me questions and laughed a raspy joy. But her cadence was a melody I couldn't grasp, her way of speaking impossible for me to follow. My pauses were awkward and my embarrassment apparent until we settled into a strange back and forth in which Dawn translated a new English for me.

Sophomore year, the year President Reagan was shot, Mark lived one floor below me. He called me by my last name, which he didn't say right, but I didn't care. He was tall, Black, and funny, and taken with everything I said. "You're almost white, Khan," he'd tease, and I'd say, "Almost doesn't make me white." That same year, I had a friend who was as white as white can be, with platinum blond hair to punctuate it. Vicky's mother worked in a factory, her stepfather too. She invited me to her home for a weekend, and since she lived close to where Dawn planned to be, I asked if she could join us for a night. Vicky was quick to turn me down, announcing her mother wouldn't allow a Black person in the house. I struggled to tell Dawn. Her eyes widened for only a moment before years of practice made her smile and sigh, "That's okay." Fifteen years later, and no word in between, I received an email when I was in Islamabad from Vicky who was

in India, spending a few months of her family's year-long sab-
batical around the world. She inquired about visiting Pakistan,
and I offered our home if she decided to visit Islamabad, which
she accepted. Later that year, I received our only holiday card
from her, which included a form letter account of their travels.
I skimmed it for Pakistan and did not recognize the country she
visited nor the people she met.

In graduate school, during President Reagan's second term,
my closest friend was Indian American, her parents immigrants
from Calcutta. I'd cut my long hair and we went to the annual
Halloween party looking like punks with spiked hair, wearing
tight jeans with "I'm a Republican" patches on the pockets, a
costume we thought hysterical for reasons now unknown. She
was deep brown, and me, virtually white beside her. Graduate
school, less than a year behind us, seemed remote when I visited her for respite after I'd left a job in DC. Naeem and I already
planned to marry, and as we talked about the future, she was
matter of fact in her prediction. If Naeem and I stayed in the US,
our children would have difficulty in the schools. She had, her
brother had, and my kids would be no different. "You know that,
right?" she said as I tried to make sense of what she'd said. I didn't
believe her. Anti-miscegenation laws had come and gone, schools
were integrated, mindsets were altered. "You'll see," she giggled
at my confusion, but I didn't. Naeem was dark year-round, I was
browner in the summer. Given my parents, I knew how color
worked. My children would be lighter than Naeem, and saved
from her prediction.

•

I shared little with my mother about the boys' troubles, as if it
were my failing that had caused them, or, in comparison to what
she'd endured—world war—their experiences were trifles. But
when I'd been in college, I told her that no one (except the for-

eigners, and there were only seven of us in my year) knew where Pakistan was, which made her shake her head. "The stupidity," she said, which is what I muttered to myself when my children told me their classmates, too, were hopeless with geography.

Kamal's memories are scattered, but he remembers the school's atlas open to the page where his parents grew up, countries fit together like puzzle pieces and wandering across the binding.

Immediately after 9/11, and hardly a week into Kamal's fourth-grade year, air traffic was grounded, but sometimes military aircraft flew above Ithaca anyway. During recess one day, children noticed an airplane, and Jim, the largest boy on the playground, was suddenly enraged. He picked up a rock and threw it like a baseball as hard as he could at the sky. "Go home, you Afghanistanis," he shouted, running after the plane and, unwittingly, into the trajectory of the falling rock.

The school social worker said that students had been traumatized by 9/11. I told her that my children were aware that while their cousins slept in Karachi, US military aircraft flew overhead on the way to bombing runs in Afghanistan. She didn't know what to do with this, so I did not mention the Tomahawk missiles launched from ships and sailing over Karachi at night. After more threats and thrown punches, Kamal and Gunner were put in an office around a table with a huge atlas. With the world between them, they were shown facts: Pakistan was Pakistan, Afghanistan was Afghanistan, the two were not the same. Then, as now, Kamal felt the geography lesson was wasted. Countries that end with -stan might as well be the same. They are mispronounced as much as they are mistrusted, misunderstood and mixed up, especially on a playground in the middle of a central New York morning. Presumably, had Pakistan and Afghanistan been one and the same, the boys wouldn't have gathered around an open atlas for a geography lesson, and Ter-rist, easy and concise like a nickname, would still have slipped from children's mouths.

Naeem remembers a meeting a year earlier. He'd taken Kamal back to school at the end of the day to pick up a forgotten item. The corridor outside the third-grade classrooms was covered floor to ceiling in hand-colored drawings of US flags taped to the wall and stacked like blocks into wide towers. "What's this?" Naeem asked. Kamal explained that each third grader had drawn a flag of where they were from. Arranged into columns by country, the flags were a math lesson in bar graphs. Kamal had told his teacher he came from more than one place and wasn't sure which flag to draw. She said that since he was born in Syracuse, he should draw a US flag. He asked if he could draw a flag that was half American and half Pakistani, but neither halves nor quarters, only wholes were permitted.

The corridor display prompted Naeem to talk with the teacher. He sat across from her on a child's chair around a low table, in sight of a Dale Earnhardt NASCAR poster on her refrigerator, and asked about the purpose of a bar graph almost entirely made up of US flags. Mrs. David's response was to warn him that he was intruding on her beliefs and end the conversation. Halfway through the school year, after a hallway fight, Kamal discovered Tae Kwon Do. Dale Earnhardt was dead by then and Mrs. David had held a moment of silence for him and cried.

I remember a letter, but not what we wrote until I find a copy by accident. Over time, the incidents on the playground and on the bus and in the hallways multiplied, and we finally responded with a letter to the principal, copied to the district administration, chronicling the many incidents of racism and the school's ineffective response. It was too late by then, as Kamal was about to graduate from elementary school, and our letter made little difference for Shahid, four years behind him, who became a stand-in for similar treatment. Four years later, when the boys once again attended the same school together, both of them had become Tae Kwon Do black belts. On the school bus one afternoon, an unsuspecting older boy threw a Snapple bottle at Shahid. Shahid picked it up and threw it back hard, causing the bus driver to pull off the road, Kamal to intervene, and me to be their driver for the length of their suspension which lasted the rest of the year. They'd become a force, those brothers (at least when they weren't fighting each other), a kinship grown from being brown.

When Kamal was fifteen, the Iraq war surge began; by this time both boys were safe in the public school district's alternative school. One afternoon, I heard a *This American Life* episode which featured a Palestinian family whose daughter was mercilessly bullied in fourth grade after 9/11. The story was terrifying, the boys' hardly notable beside it. I sent Kamal the podcast and a few days later asked him what he thought. He laughed and shook his head.

"Mama, that girl must have really done something," he said.

"What do you mean?" I asked.

"No one gets treated like that unless they ask for it."

And I saw how deeply certain lessons settled.

•

The boys' elementary school is nothing like my childhood school. Theirs sits in a sea of green in an unremarkable corner of a US college town. Nearby, but out of sight, is the south end of Cayuga Lake, as are the area's gorges through which Fall Creek runs, and the university's rolling golf course, equestrian research facility, and Lab of Ornithology. The red brick school is a ten-minute walk from our home, and on approach it sinks away from the road into an amalgamation of three single-story buildings, and then into wood chipped playgrounds, asphalt basketball courts, and manicured fields that follow a suburban street lined with mown lawns and two-car garages of single-family homes.

Our school, too, had been red brick and single story. It was located in sector H-9 in the outskirts of Islamabad, and reaching it required a forty-five-minute bus ride that traversed a busy Peshawar Road and a few empty, unpaved streets. I didn't realize the shining yellow of our bus was distinctive of US school buses until I arrived in the US. The only lake in the vicinity was Rawal Lake, the artificial reservoir that supplies the city's water, and the dominant green was the Margalla Hills that are the north border of the city. The closest residential dwellings were fashioned from mud and dung, homes to barefoot children who chased our school buses for fun when they were not watching animals graze on adjoining arid patches of land.

For years, the only fact about our school that interested our children is that Naeem and I had ridden the same school bus. Later, the children's curiosity in our school was renewed when they learned about the events of 1979, when six people were killed (two Americans and four Pakistanis) during an attack on the US embassy, reducing it to smoldering ruins. Both Naeem and I had graduated by then, but the school was also attacked, and instead of a raging crowd and fire, a few dozen miscreants jumped the boundary wall and terrorized students, leaving the buildings and everyone in them to survive. Twelve years later, in the early 1990s, Naeem and I returned to visit the school for the first time, and the guards at the gate sprang from their chairs to shake our hands and welcome us home. In one of Naeem's photographs, I'm alone in the parking lot in the shade of a tree I don't remember. Pregnant with Kamal, I stand beside an old school bus, now painted baby blue to match the local buses, the school's name buried under years of paint.

In 2014, on a rushed trip to Islamabad that my mother was too sick to join us on, I visited the school with Shahid before Kamal joined us for the week. It took us much longer than expected to get there, and after getting lost in the surrounding maze, our car passed through a black and yellow security barrier that resembled a parking garage gate, except for being fortified, the wrong colors, and manned by three armed men. Finally, we arrived at a huge wall topped with barbed wire extending away from it, seemingly impossible to breach. Atop the wall was a watchtower, a sentry post near the gate not unlike the one at Elmira Correctional Facility, a maximum-security prison in Elmira, New York, where Naeem and a friend had taught a class. The tower guards stood to either side of a mounted assault rifle and paid close attention while we walked single file to the final security checkpoint. Waiting for us in the cramped room was a metal detector, the largest armed chowkidar I've ever seen, and a Pakistani woman who took our phones and checked our IDs against a list. Just beyond lay the first familiar sight, the school's original perimeter wall. I remembered when a single guard at the open gate used to sit in a bamboo chair nodding in and out of sleep while an unloaded rifle rested between his knees as traffic came and went.

The campus was as congested as the roads leading up to it— as if in the years since I'd graduated, the school had spared no expense with every possible amenity, including a new cafeteria, several tennis courts, and a large swimming pool. Our guide was the school's registrar, a young American woman who blushed with excitement when she said that her husband, whom I imagined a US marine, was about to be posted to Bangkok. She said tuition was $18,000 a year, and the school population was 75% Pakistani, with the balance being foreign and the most recent enrollees French and German. It took a moment for me to absorb the numbers and to understand that the mostly American school of my childhood was now mostly Pakistani. She waved at the swimming pool behind a locked fence, and I had difficulty placing it on the map of the school that I carried in my mind. Had the spot been a parking lot? A field? The location of a makeshift stall that sold Fanta? I ran my hand along the wire fence as I tried to orient myself, and Shahid pointed to a stack of cricket pads in my path. The used pads were gray with sweat and dull grass stains, the shape of children's legs preserved in the way they lay. I asked the guide for confirmation that students played cricket. Her response was swift—boys and girls had been playing cricket, Pakistan's national sport, at the school for years. "Since when?" I balked, unable to reconcile my experience of the school with the anomaly of cricket and Pakistani boys, especially those nearby who eyed me suspiciously.

Our school did not offer cricket. We had played flag football, soccer, basketball, softball, and field hockey. In those days, the spare quads of the school emptied into vast fields that spread in all directions until they hit the easily scalable boundary wall, on the other side of which grew wild marijuana plants. We trained in sweltering heat on the track around the fields, a grueling activity that sometimes gave me leg cramps, the severity of which once helped me describe labor contractions to a friend.

At the end of our tour, I noticed that the parking lot was filled with sleek white buses rather than the yellow ones of my childhood or my children's in Ithaca. I recalled the long-ago afternoon bus rides when boys spat on pedestrians and bicyclists, and I was never brave enough to ask them to stop or tell my parents because I feared being pulled from the school. We drove home by an alternate route on which I immediately found my bearings. I saw that the mud dwellings near the school had been replaced with a tent village, home to refugees from the massive earthquake years earlier or, perhaps, from Pakistani army efforts to drive the Taliban from the northern areas. Children, much like the ones who'd chased our buses, played between rows of battered tents and faded blue UN tarps and, on a school day, were not in school.

On the drive home, I asked Shahid if he'd noticed cricket bats or if we'd seen a cricket pitch. He hadn't, but I said, "Are you sure?" I remembered something then: being seventeen and at college when my aunt called to tell me that the embassy and the school my sister, Ayesha, still attended had been attacked, and the newscast I listened to on my shortwave radio announced that students fought off their attackers with cricket bats. That could not be true, I thought at the time, because the school only had baseball bats. The inaccuracy seized me then, and now, decades later, soiled cricket pads shaped by knees and shins lying against the swimming pool fence brought it back all over again.

•

The day after the November 8, 2016, election (the results of which my mother would never know), Shahid and I speak on the telephone.

"I'm so worried about you and your brother," I say.

"Why?" he asks, and I think he's joking.

"Because of the registry!"

He laughs his deepest laugh and tells me not to worry so much. He says they are already registered, have been since 9/11, or perhaps earlier.

I think about it for a moment because, after all, a post-9/11 registry had existed for years. "But it will be more dangerous for you now," I insist.

When I share my concerns with Kamal, who lives in Europe now, he is equally amused. As I listen to his banter, I'm tempted to abandon my worries, if only for a moment, but then he refers to the US as Trumpistan and his gallows humor unnerves me. I'm conditioned by years of media coverage about Pakistan and Afghanistan and Kazakhstan and all the other -stans of the world, and alongside the president-elect's platform, Trumpistan can only be a place of fear. Soon enough, the inauguration happens, and I check our passports for expiration dates. We submit them for renewal on my birthday, hours before the travel ban is announced. Pakistan is not yet on the list of countries, but I know how easily it could be, perhaps as soon as tomorrow. Every day I wait for our postman, and every day that our passports don't arrive, my knot of worry grows.

It's cold in the crowded waiting area of Syracuse's railway station, where we're whiling away a delay before Shahid returns to college after Thanksgiving break. A young man no older than Shahid, military-issued bags at his feet, also waits, and I wonder which war he is off to. I recall my mother's surprise on her post-9/11 visits to the US. She was puzzled by the preponderance of flags—in windows, on doors, flying from houses and cars—as if people needed to be reminded of where they were. She'd never seen such a phenomenon, even in World War II. As we drove her through the countryside, up and down beautiful hills, past young wineries and neatly fenced farms without a single person in sight and the sweet fragrance of cut grass all about, she'd remark, "You'd never know this country was at war." Next to me in the train station, loud music escapes Shahid's earphones and I see him as if I'm the stranger sitting across from us. I tell him to pull the hoodie from his head and he rolls his eyes, but obliges. Kamal is flying home soon and, as if he doesn't already know, I remind myself to tell him to shave for Immigration and to keep handy the telephone numbers of our attorney friend, so that if he is detained and allowed a telephone call, they are at his fingertips. He has been singled out on travels and has seen the inside of special waiting rooms, so he knows that Immigration is its own country where officers not travel documents reign supreme.

We cannot speak of blessings conferred by 9/11, but there is one. We owe our children's complex selves to those events and the aftermath. Bar graphs, *America the Beautiful,* and the abundance of US flags have prevented our sons from fully assimilating—they are not entirely at home here. If I were still in touch with my Indian American friend, I'd tell her that she was right and I was wrong. But our sons understand something we wanted them to know: there is a world larger than them out there, and most of it is full of color. They straddle worlds. Not quite like us, but not unlike us. Once in a while, I remind my sons that I'm half white and I put my arms beside their much larger ones to make my point. They shake their heads and feign exasperation, even when I insist that my mix makes them one quarter white. In this country, in these *America First* times, they are brown.

•

I do not know what my parents saw when they observed their three children, who were other than them. My father, having grown up in Lahore during British rule, might have marveled that his children were lighter than he, but it's not likely that he had a category in mind for us. When he arrived in 1950s Raleigh, North Carolina, for his graduate education to *Whites Only* and *Colored Only* water fountains, he calculated he was neither and did not use water fountains. If his confusion persisted, North Carolina's anti-miscegenation laws cleared up the matter when it prevented my parents from marrying there. Decades later, when asked to recall the first white woman he'd known, he remembered a young woman in Lahore, about his age, in the apartment above who'd return from playing tennis in a skirt. When asked if he'd ever spoken to her, his horrified "Oh, no!" was immediate, as if he hadn't later married a white woman and had children with her.

I never asked my mother, but I imagine that it thrilled her to have children who were darker than she in the way it had thrilled me when a baby boy (twice!) came out of my body. Giving birth to a different sex, making what wasn't me, was mind-bending, another miracle of childbirth, which is how giving birth to brown children might also have been for her.

Although we were darker than my mother, my siblings and I were varied shades of brown, which my mother, growing up in Amsterdam, would have always known was possible. My brother is lightest of all and when my mother rushed him to her mother's hospital bedside the day after he was born, her mother must have been surprised at a grandchild almost as pale as she. I'm darker than my brother and sister, and in summer their color, like my children's now, didn't overlap with mine. The three of us were the closest my mother would get to being brown, and along with my father and living in Islamabad, the most distance she could put between herself and the flat country of Holland.

TWO

Decades ago, in July of 1958, my mother Thera arrived in Pakistan for the first time. My parents traveled from Southampton to Karachi by ship, but she was never more nauseous than when she climbed the rolling stairs on the airport tarmac to board the flight to Lahore. She was slow on her swollen feet, marveling at her mother's warning of the heat that awaited her in this far-off land. Already drenched in perspiration, the long hair she would cut after Omar, my brother, was born was unbearable on her back. Her mother had been right: the heat was like steam rushing from the spout of a boiling kettle. My father, Munir, stopped to help her up the stairs. She liked to believe that she was the reason for their trip, but the urgency went beyond my father's desire to introduce his bride to family. In order to begin their new lives, he needed to secure bureaucratic permissions to accept a UN job offer.

It was true that my twenty-four-year-old mother already knew a thing or two about leaving one country for another. She'd done it the first time when she left Amsterdam for Chicago, where my parents lay on the shore of Lake Michigan and recited poetry to each other. In the long-distance relationship that followed, detailed in the eighteen months of correspondence that I will find several years later, my parents weigh their love against the realities that await them. In one of his letters, my father warns that Pakistan (*So poor!*) would not be familiar to her. Sitting in the airplane to Lahore as it taxis down the runway, perhaps she recalled their exchange. *Munir, my love, you ask if I can do without,* she writes, and tells him that she can.

None of us can do without 5 Queen's Road. It is a simple address, a single house, that awaits her in Lahore. It is our beginning of Pakistan.

Five Queen's Road didn't belong to her in-laws, even if they behaved as if it did. She learned the house was partitioned shortly before British India was, in 1947. The border that cleaved the country produced the independent nations of India and Pakistan; the border that cleaved the house shifted, growing or shrinking depending on perspective and the passage of time. It had been built by the British and eventually sold to a Hindu, Dina Nath, whose family decided against leaving Lahore for India after Partition. Instead, Dina Nath converted to Islam, drew a line down the middle of the house, and searched for a Muslim tenant to live on the other side, hoping that the presence of a Muslim might protect him from the raging violence against Hindus who had dared remain in Pakistan. My grandparents, their children, a parent, and several siblings moved in. For reasons that are unclear and now impossible to know, my grandfather and Dina Nath grew to dislike each other until eventually the men stopped speaking and the house crumbled under the weight of their feud. The women remained friends, forgiving each other's trespasses, like the time my aunt forgot to invite her friend from across the way to her child's birthday party. The men blamed each other for every new crack in the wall and leak in the roof, and neither would make repairs. A single exception was the replacement of an in-ground toilet with a Western-style toilet bowl and flush, in deference to Thera and her first visit. My mother observed the feud with genuine curiosity; all she had to compare it to was the Catholic and Protestant divide in her own country or the Black and white one in America.

My mother had plenty of time to contemplate her new surroundings, for which neither the places she'd visited nor the books she'd read prepared her. Her mother-in-law was busy from morning to night managing the household, her sisters-in-law attended university, her brothers-in-law tended to their own family responsibilities, and my father was off chasing paperwork. Despite the grandness of what a Queen's Road address might suggest, the house was not that at all. In fact, the home which awaited my mother was not a house, but a portion of one. It was two bedrooms and bathrooms, a dining room with three entrances, a living room which doubled as a makeshift bedroom at night, a study, and, for some mysterious reason, the entire back lawn, of which a corner was an outside kitchen where my grandmother prepared all meals. The walls were white and empty, an absence of abundance she might have felt keenly because her childhood walls had been full of paintings. A sister-in-law's watercolor leaned on the marble mantel beside a bronze *Allah,* which together made up the dining room's only adornments. In slides of that visit, my mother is resplendent, her smile radiant with the happiness of a new bride and expectant mother, brimming with the confidence of someone unbothered by unfamiliar and modest surroundings.

My grandfather was a high-court judge and presided over disputes larger than the one that governed his home. He looked the part as a stern and rail-thin man who towered over everyone, even my mother. There is no kind way to say that he was feared. My mother said his grown sons stood when he entered a room and, if they happened to be smoking, expertly hid still-glowing cigarettes behind their backs. He didn't tolerate being contradicted and would shout down anyone who dared to disagree with him. Thera, however, wasn't deterred, either in private or public, and my grandfather, to everyone's surprise, did not mind.

While others went about their daily routines, my grandfather sometimes carried his after-lunch tea to where my mother lay alone in the garden trying to overcome another wave of nausea. They built a friendship that allowed her to say what she thought ("Not always, mind you," she would later recall). This, too, despite the consternation of other family members, not to mention her new husband.

"We don't do that here," Munir would say, a confident *here* which was interchangeable with Pakistan, as if the country had existed forever and not just a decade.

My mother and my grandfather discussed my aunt's desire to paint, a pastime that my grandfather did not support. When my mother saw that she would not change his mind, she supplied her sister-in-law with paints and brushes, which she insisted my father scour the Lahore markets for that first visit, but on all subsequent trips, she would buy and carry from Vienna to Lahore.

My grandfather's profession must have set Thera, the granddaughter of a Dutch *notaris*, at ease. She was accustomed to her grandfather's office filled with law books and the mammoth desks built to hold them, which she frequented when she wandered through the first floor of his home in Maastricht on the River Maas. Like her own grandfather, the sheer volume of my grandfather's work was evident in the hours he kept and in the chaos of his study, where all surfaces and much of the floor were permanently covered. Perhaps her familiarity helped the two become friends. She, however, loved the man before she arrived in Lahore and saw the desk from which he wrote the letter that granted his son permission to marry her. *We have all decided to seek our genuine pleasure in your sweet pleasure,* he wrote in the brief missive to my father in Chicago, forwarded to where she waited in Amsterdam.

My grandmother was nothing like Oma, my mother's grandmother, yet my mother was loved by her all the same, and the fact that neither spoke each other's language appeared not to matter.

"Your mother told me . . . ," Thera would say to Munir that summer and forever after.

Early on, he would check with his mother, who'd confirm it.

"How did you tell her?" he'd ask his mother.

"How did she tell you?" he'd ask his wife.

My grandmother's voice was soft, and her laugh caught in a child's giggle when she looked across the dining room table and her eyes fell on my father (or another of her children) and lingered, relishing his very being. She'd survived a difficult mother-in-law, too many brothers-in-law, the death of a child, the births of eight children, and a band of grandchildren, some of whom would one day visit from the other side of the world. My mother, who was Catholic before converting to Islam and marrying my father, said she was a saint. Certainly the daily menu of chicken curry, keema, dals, and chutneys my grandmother produced was saintly, as were the chapattis, slathered with butter and rolled in sugar, with which she tried to tempt my mother, who was unable to ingest much. At family meals on the ample sheesham table that magically expanded to seat any number of guests at a moment's notice, my mother must have looked out at the sea of faces she did not know, wondrous of the ready-made family she'd found thousands of miles from her broken one. In contrast with her father who'd absconded with a mistress and her brokenhearted mother who was convalescing from tuberculosis, 5 Queen's Road made her long more than ever to make her own family. Five or six months later, when my parents left for Vienna and my father's UN job, she cried to leave the place behind.

When I first arrived as a child, the bad blood between the two sides of the divided house was a physical presence, there in the stale air we breathed. It was sometimes possible to decipher a few words in the Punjabi-Urdu-English lexicon of my uncles, enough to understand something of the latest disagreement. Dina Nath had sold off parcels of the property to car shops that set up in the front lawn. He lavished bribes on the sweepers, so that they would extend their homes into the narrow driveway. But the man was invisible, a remarkable feat for the person responsible for all our misery. My mother was not sure if she had ever seen him, but my aunts told stories of early sightings:

when the families still shared the back patio, they had seen Dina Nath's wife serving her husband food.

The large yellow bungalow existed in a stranglehold. A mess of car repair shops extended from the road to the house and decimated what my father said had once been carefully tended terraces of flowers. The semi-permanent structures had tarps for doors and tires for walls, and heaps of tools were scattered in pockets between the broken cars. With a generosity that enraged my grandfather because it presupposed they belonged there, the owners volunteered to fix our car and bicycle tires free of charge. At the opposite side of the property, the sweepers' colony was a dense adobe village. It was home to hundreds of sweepers, most of them descendants of pre-Partition Dalits who had converted to Christianity to escape the limitations of their caste, only to remain trapped by their livelihood. The colony had expanded into the driveway, until all that remained between the boundary wall and the car shops was an alley too narrow to accommodate more than a single vehicle at a time. No one could say when either first appeared, only that Dina Nath was to blame.

To stand on the flat roof of the large yellow bungalow was to witness 5 Queen's Road's demise. In the distance you could see where the traffic on the street ended and a mess of car repair shops extended from the road to the house, and also the sweepers' mud wall. Almost two stories closer to the sky, the roof was a refuge, an open expanse mercifully free of adults. Up there we violated the line separating our family from the other with reckless abandon, drawing colorful chalked squares for our hopscotch games and jumping up and over onto Dina Nath's side. We collected broken glass as if it were lost treasure and once recovered frayed twine from an abandoned laundry line to play a string game we didn't know was called cat's cradle. We danced and jumped on the Hindu family's portion of the house in a game of dare that kept us busy for hours. Too late, my mother would become aware of our mischief and race up the steep concrete stairs brilliantly concealed in a seam in our side of the house. When she was furious because we'd interrupted her reading, she'd give us a shout, and when she was less energetic and more resigned, she inquired without inflection, "What in God's name are you doing?" only to sit down and join us. Either reaction put a firm but temporary stop to our fun.

So long as my grandfather wasn't home, his study was my preferred entrance to the house. During the Christmas holidays, his doorway framed an elaborate nativity scene across the way, which I could look in on if I broke the rules and sat behind my grandfather's two enormous desks, one directly behind the other. The backdrop was an extra wall just long enough to hide the entrance to the sweepers' colony. The scene always included the same yellow plastic Jesus in a rickety hay-filled manger and strings of furiously blinking lights powered by electricity stolen from the house. All night, flashing light bounced through our closed bathroom windows and drew fleeting patterns on walls of flaking paint.

The winter I was eight or nine, the daughter of our sweeper became my favorite playmate; my sister, Ayesha, was too small, and my brother, Omar, who was three years older, had outgrown any need for me. She may have been younger by a year or two, but she was more worldly. She wore multicolored glass bangles on her wrists, had pierced ears and a delicate sparkling stud in her nose, and in my memory she wore a sheer dupatta that stayed in place on her shoulders even though she was too young for it. There was a language barrier between us, but language wasn't necessary to share the wonder of a snow globe my mother had packed or to delight in the echo of stones thrown into the barren well on the lawn. We spent most of our time playing in the prickly brown grass that grew without water or care. I'm not sure I ever knew her name. The slight girl followed her mother to work every day, intuiting when she was needed to wring out rags and return them to where her mother scrubbed toilet bowls when she wasn't sweeping carpets or washing the verandah. My friend wasn't in school, but my mother bought her a tin pencil box, notebooks, and primary school readers from Ferozesons on Mall Road. That winter she was a regular presence at the house, and, however briefly, my way into the sweepers' colony.

One morning, while our mothers were preoccupied and our fathers elsewhere, we snuck away, holding hands. She pulled me around the curiously stunted wall that hid the colony entrance and we arrived at a complicated maze of tight alleys and open sewers, which she easily navigated. As we maneuvered this way and that, all that was missing from my rooftop perspective came into sharp focus. The colony was alive with intense smells and textures: sautéing onions and raw sewage, a stray dog's scratchy coat against my knee, mud walls I grazed with my fingertips, a bristle of straw that got stuck between my toes. Kids and radios played loudly. By the time we reached the simple structure that was her home, I was out of breath, coughing dust and whatever else we had kicked up from the alleys as we ran. She was about to part the strings of beads that functioned as the door when a woman hanging laundry on an adjoining roof saw us. She dropped an armful of wet clothes and launched into a shrill tirade my mother would have called the rant of a fisherman's wife, although she didn't know any fishermen and the sea was almost seven hundred miles away. I didn't need Punjabi or Urdu to understand what was being said. The longer we stood there, the more furiously my heart pounded and the more I wanted to go home. When my friend let go of my hand, I was terrified. We'd attracted others, among them a group of small children giggling at our misfortune. The woman wagged her finger at my friend, scolding her for having led me there. At her first pause, we turned and ran as fast as we could, she barefoot, me in my flip-flops.

When we surfaced on the other side of the wall, my grandfather was waiting.

"Why did you go?"

"What were you doing?"

"Who were you with?

"What did you touch?"

"Don't you know better?"

Our transgression was poorly explained: the colony was a dangerous place in which anything could have happened to me, but apparently not to her. As punishment, I spent the afternoon confined to my grandparents' room, where only my grandmother bothered to check on me, and although I heard my mother say, "For goodness sakes, let the child out!" to my father when he returned home, she didn't dare challenge my grandfather on this. My grandmother recited prayers while kissing my head. When she left, I entertained myself by snooping through the tiny dresser drawers on either side of the mirror. I played with a pharmacist's small envelopes, folded from newspaper and filled with chalky pills. My friend took her time returning to 5 Queen's Road, and when she did, she had other things to do than play with me.

Until the sweet scent of teak rose in my bedroom decades later and on another continent, I'd almost forgotten our adventure. My mother had inherited my grandmother's dresser first, but when my father died and our family home dissolved, it crossed the world in a shipping container and became mine. I unpacked it alone, my young children distracted by something else. After I cut the twine and tore away layers of packaging securing the mirror, I opened and closed the two tiny drawers. It took me a moment to identify the earthy fragrance as ancient teak, but when I did, I remembered this: on that long-ago day, my friend's shalwar kameez was maroon, her single plait was braided with a thin gold ribbon stained with hair oil, her hand was rough and solid in mine. As always, her silver-soled feet were silent on the ground.

•

The house had once been grand and beautiful, and there were still hints of this in the ruin. The ceilings were sky-high, and there were narrow clerestories in the bedrooms, as if someone had had the foresight to know that the outside walls would do well to be fortified rather than interrupted by standard windows. Every so often, a sparrow flew through a broken clerestory (they were all broken by the time I arrived there) and while trying furiously to escape, left warm gray-white droppings on our bedding. Ceiling fans on long chains swayed just enough to frighten us as we lay watching the grimy blades whip up a breeze. The walls were so thick that it was almost impossible for a child standing with her chest to the doorframe to grip them on either side.

The dining room table ran parallel to a built-in cupboard with glass doors behind which my mother stored oval tins of chocolate-covered almonds she brought as gifts and we filched. In a corner sat a wooden cabinet laden with wire baskets of fruit and jute bags of rice, the supplies poorly protected from swarming flies by flimsy screen doors that failed to latch. The bathroom door also had a broken latch. That room offered the only privacy in our house, but even there we were not alone: our constant companions were black carpenter ants thick enough to crunch like cockroaches. They came regardless of how many times the floor was scrubbed and soaked with Dettol, even when my mother did it herself.

My mother once told a story of an afternoon when she left me in a wooden playpen on the patio in my grandfather's care. He watched over me from behind a stack of newspapers and a gurgling hookah. An eagle (or vulture, depending on who is telling the story) circled above, and when it swooped down to grab me, my grandfather looked up from his newspaper and jumped into the playpen in one continuous motion. For the most part, though, he had little time and few words for anyone, his grandchildren included. Sometimes, if we were present at the breakfast table while he drank his tea, and he noticed us lift our faces in his direction as he left, he paused to plant a wet kiss on our foreheads. He did his fair share of bellowing, but every so often he'd catch us by surprise. Safely out of adult earshot, he'd ask in hushed tones: "Going somewhere?" In these moments he smiled with his eyes closed, and wiggled his ears to our delight.

My grandmother combed her striking white hair into a tight bun, and as she aged and her hair thinned, the teeth of her comb left behind wider lines of scalp. Her waking hours were spent low to the ground, either on a prayer carpet in private communion with God or crouched on a wooden piri, preparing the next meal. Sometimes she invited us to help clean the rice and lentils. We dropped beside her to pick out tiny stones and bits of dried pods, before dragging the heavy bowls across the stone floor to the spigot to fill them with water. Together, we swirled rice and lentils between our fingers until the water ran clean or we lost interest. Afternoon light danced on the rippling water in the tins and our hands melted into hers.

She had age spots and wrinkled hands and raised veins that crisscrossed her ankles. She was concealed in white cotton shalwars and lightly printed kameezes, and I was left to imagine her elbows and knees. But there were other ways to know her body. During lazy afternoons, when she chose not to retire to her room for a nap, my grandmother lay face down on the living room floor (without the benefit of our thin mattresses rolled up and tucked in a corner) and waited for me to notice. She'd taught me to massage her by walking on her, and I mastered a side-step shuffle that began on her buttocks and ended at the end of one leg before starting back up the other. Walking on her legs was like navigating a living balance beam; I fought until the last second, arms flailing, finally falling and waiting for my grandmother to indicate where she wanted me to begin again. She groaned with joy as I sank my weight into her, and I can still summon the odd intimacy. Her buttocks were jelly, slipping underneath as I attempted to gain a foothold. Her tiny calves were mostly bone.

The delicate groove behind her knee was designed for my child-hood feet. I remember dropping to a crouch to check on her when she went quiet or her eyes stayed closed for too long, and my head scraping my grandfather's stack of *Reader's Digest* which were always the same and my mother, Omar, and I all read. Near her face I felt whispers of prayer, but I still worried that my feet had kneaded the life out of her.

No matter what time of day we left Lahore or how delayed our departure, my grandmother's farewell ritual could not be hur-ried. She prayed continuously as the car was loaded and we hugged aunts, uncles, and cousins. My mother held on to my grandmother who seemed ever smaller in her fold. She was last to embrace us, and she nodded and smiled her goodbye without interrupting her recitation from the Quran. We swallowed a pinch of sugar from her hand that she'd begun praying over before we'd gathered. Palms cupped, she blew her prayers in our direction, confident they would follow us through the sorry lane that wound along the sweepers' colony and into Queen's Road—and onward, into our other lives.

•

I last saw 5 Queen's Road on a visit with my father in the 1980s, during a summer I was home from graduate school. My mother, who thought we were mad to drive all the way to Lahore and all the way back to visit a place that no longer existed, said so before we left our home in Islamabad.

"What? You're driving five hours each way for one night?"

"Never mind," my father said. "I have things to do in Lahore as well."

"You're taking her? You could just go there yourself with your camera!"

"I want to go," I said.

"Why don't you come with us, darling?" my father asked.

"Come on, Munno! To see an empty plot of land? To check it's still there?!"

My father laughed with her.

"You're worried you'll forget the place? You think that's possible?" she asked me.

I did not. I didn't yet know how memory worked, that things you think you'll never forget are gone one day, and mundane ones, like the sound of the gas water heater coming on in 5 Queen's Road, never leave you.

"I want to see it for myself," I said, because when I learned that the house had disappeared, vanished brick by brick into truck after truck, taken to who knows where to be reused who knows how, it seemed impossible.

The house had been demolished, and in its place was a neatly demarcated but vacant piece of land. A single wire secured its borders, distinguishing it from the car shop settlement and sweepers' colony. That January day, the barren plot was dusted green and appeared too small to ever have accommodated a crumbling house and two warring families. While my father and a car shop owner embraced, I turned my back to where the house had stood and where the broken well and unremarkable tree still did, and tried to take in 5 Queen's Road. Without the vantage point of the roof, I could see far less. The crush of the car shop settlement had abated and a new alley-cum-driveway that veered away from the mud wall meant I could not find the entrance to the sweepers' colony. Chaos, it seemed, had given way to a quiet peace.

Soon after our visit, my grandparents died, almost nine months apart, my grandfather one January, and my grandmother the following September, when to their dismay, both my parents were visiting Vienna. My mother accompanied my father to Schwechat airport, where they begged for a flight home. Across the counter, two airline attendants bantered about helping a *Schwarzer* until my mother sent my father to buy a newspaper and used her flawless German to put them in their place and secure a reservation. My father arrived home too late for his mother's funeral, but he needn't have worried because they are all together now in Miani Sahib's graveyard, where my father's parents are finally the same size. Evidence of their lives surrounds them: their sons' graves, the graves of a daughter-in-law and two grandsons. While their bodies shriveled and shrank into the earth, the battle for 5 Queen's Road continued to rage: in a decades-long court case, my grandfather's family used Partition evacuee property regulations to fight for the land. Dina Nath's family fought to maintain full ownership, and the car repair shops built a case, too, based on possession. In the end, Dina Nath's family maintained rights to one-third of the property, which contained an easement to the main road; the car shop settlement was given ownership of what had been the front lawn; and my father and his siblings were awarded what remained, but without an easement, it was worth less and, anyway, my father was soon dead.

I must have imagined that my grandparents took 5 Queen's Road with them, because after their deaths and before writing the place into reexistence in a novel that shared its name, it rarely came to mind. The exception was when I visited Lahore and used the address to locate myself, as if the house were true north.

"Well, it was!" my mother said unsurprised, when I confided this to her.

No matter where I was in the city, I went out of my way to pass through what was renamed Fatima Jinnah Road. With Naeem and our children, too, I tried to find what was the house, but each time I'd been away too long, the landscape of the road had changed too much, and there was no one to ask, as almost everyone is gone. Always, I'd wave in the direction of one commercial parking lot, or another, and pretend the gesture was not a guess.

THREE

Islamabad, too, begins with a house. It is my first memory of Islamabad, my beginning of the place. It is not where we will live when we move to Pakistan from Vienna in June of 1972, but it is the house my father insists on building in the 1960s, imagining that such a move will happen in our family's future. I'm seven or eight during that December visit and wearing a new red dress when my father lines up the three of us for a photograph. He has posed us in front of the unfinished house, and behind him, as he handles the camera, I can see the sky above the Margalla Hills. The house has walls but no roof, and there is nothing on either side or behind it. It's an island, as if the land coughed it up half made. All of us—the city, the house, the mother, the father, and their three children—are frozen in a moment of becoming.

Islamabad was still young, like us, when my father moved us there a few years later when I was ten, and it already had ghosts. Pakistan had a new leader, Zulfikar Ali Bhutto, but the country had just lost a war and half its landmass when Bangladesh was born. Although the war was fought a thousand miles away in what was East Pakistan, there were signs of it in the capital. Streets and houses rose up daily in the rush to build a capital on the empty plain, but not far from where we lived was an older house whose work had halted midway. A manual concrete mixer stuck out of its side, and a half balcony hung from the wreck. Bushes filled holes where windows ought to have been. Concrete stairs rose up or fell down without reaching the ground or the roof. Goats grazed on floors of weeds, and doorways were splattered with animal excrement. The house stood near the intersection of Hill and Margalla roads and whenever I passed it on bicycle or by foot, I sprinted because it frightened me so. The East Pakistani owners had fled during the 1971 war, never to return after an independent Bangladesh was born. The detail folded into my child's universe. We'd moved to the city while sensible folk fled, and left in their wake houses haunted by animals and ghosts, one or the other bound to snatch me away.

I don't know if my mother noticed that house. She was already gone when I thought to ask her what she had seen, at only thirty-five, the first time she laid eyes on those few square miles that pretended at being a capital. By then she'd lived in Amsterdam, Chicago, and Vienna, which meant that once she landed in Islamabad, she'd been thrown across three continents. When my grandfather visited us from 5 Queen's Road, my mother shared his assessment: the place was a village, if that. Other cities had culture, "Museums, for instance," my mother would say, and they had water. She was used to the Dutch canals or Lake Michigan or the Danube, but Islamabad only had Rawal Lake, a reservoir she hardly thought worthy of visits. But it had the Margalla Hills, the foothills to the Himalayas that she grew to love. Islamabad was more promise than embodiment—of water, mountains, city, and, for my mother, another life. Not everything, however, was foreign. She was greeted with ration cards for flour and sugar, as if she'd brought along Amsterdam and remnants of her war.

For me, the city is a map of memory, a grid in which I store my life. It is rectangles organized by letters and numbers, as if C. A. Doxiadis, the city's Greek architect, believed endless, labeled combinations would bode well for the city and for us. Our sector was F-6/2, our street was 19, and our house was on a slope that dropped like a playground slide into Hill Road. In the dark it was possible to misjudge the corner, which is what happened when a school friend borrowed my new bicycle and fell off the road into a small ravine, bent the bicycle frame, and broke her collar-bone. Hill Road, wider than most, was a border between sectors. Trees that would one day be cut down for reasons no one would understand ran along the road's divider to separate oncoming traffic. They were still there when I was fourteen and a friend and I drove his motorbike up and down the road, sometimes on the correct side of the divider and sometimes not, while unknown to me my father watched from our verandah. When I returned home alone (and by foot) and he asked if I'd been on the motor-bike, I lied and vexed him further. Hill Road was also the site of a small mosque that would one day be moved, but before then, it doubled as the prearranged location of a bench at which I would meet a boyfriend when I was fifteen, creeping out of the house past incredulous chowkidars before sneaking back in.

The Margalla Hills anchored me; I was never lost if I pointed my bicycle in their direction. The city held few landmarks for me otherwise. One was my school, the International School of Islamabad, a series of quads in an H-9 sector beyond *Zero Point,* which is the exact spot in Islamabad where the axis of the planned city begins. The school was off to the left somewhere beyond a few deserted dirt roads, which was all the direction I cared to know. The other landmark was the US Embassy, closer to home, but also at a far edge of a city that disappeared into nothingness on the ground as it must have on the city's blue-prints. The embassy and school were made of the same red brick, but only the embassy was rumored to have had its bricks flown in from the US. I rarely entered the embassy, but when I did, it was into a different country in a shared landscape. You could see the Margallas arranging the sky from the swimming pool, all while imagining that the outside air was climate-controlled because that was how it felt. Dr Pepper was served on trays, US radio shows were piped in through speakers, and girls walked around in shorts and bikinis, dressed for a California beach. I tried com-ing home from soccer practice in shorts one day, prancing up the driveway with my bare legs as if it were the most natural thing to do. My father was home early from work, and I hadn't counted on his reaction.

"My God! *Where* do you think you are?" he cried. He ordered me to my room and I never tried it again.

"It's not that your shorts are too short or there is anything wrong with bare legs, but there are certain things here that we don't do in public," my Dutch mother gently reasoned, as if she'd always understood this.

We'd arrived in Pakistan by way of Karachi airport on a June day that was as hot as any. My father was late meeting us, a harbinger for how little time he would have for his family in those early days. ("Committed more to his country than his family!" my mother would complain of my father's long work hours.) After being apart for months, he wrapped us in signature bear hugs, squeezing until we couldn't breathe, but he limited his greeting for my mother to a smile, which is all he dared do publicly. She would never forgive him, and would recount what she'd said to him from her hospital bed a few weeks before her death. "What *is* this place," she fumed, "that you cannot embrace the mother of your children in front of others?"

This place was Islamabad, where much of me begins.

•

It is a stretch to say that Naeem and I met a few months later, even if it's true, but I like to think that we begin in Islamabad too. He was sixteen and I was ten, but the real difference in 1972 was that I knew his name and he didn't know mine. Neither of us knew then that our shared life would begin on a yellow school bus that belonged to the International School of Islamabad, he in the back, me in the front. His single recollection is that I was the younger sister of a soccer teammate. I have two memories of him. My first is of his wide-open grin, teeth brilliant white against his skin, while he sits with friends in the last row of bus seats. Curly hair falls in waves around his face and he carries himself with a sixteen-year-old's swagger that is electrifying to those of us whose feet barely reach the floor. *To be grown like that one day!* My second is of a photograph. He is on the front page of the school newspaper at a sports banquet where he has won an award. The paper is unnaturally white, the black and white photo too dark. He is dressed in a suit, holding a microphone, smiling shyly at his lucky girlfriend. Buried in a box, the folded newspaper accompanied him to all his cities, and ours, before it surfaced in Ithaca with a bundle of a girlfriend's drawings. My memory was accurate, except there's nothing shy about his smile.

After we are married, I will write about that time and our yellow school bus. Texans chewed tobacco and coughed up brown phlegm. Boys with oily hair spat out of windows that let in hot dry air. There might as well have been assigned seats. A young brown girl tried to make sense of it all. Some of it was true, but much of it wasn't, and plenty of what I thought was true had been transformed by memory over time and was not. I think of blond boys in the back of our bus spitting on bicyclists and pedestrians the same way I think of faded green bus seats, dirty grooves in rubber flooring, and the broken swing of the manual door opening and closing—they were always there. Naeem clarifies that this isn't true of the year we shared a bus and, in any case, certainly, the boys were not all blond. Perhaps the boys were on hiatus then.

Our time in Islamabad overlapped only a year, but even so, we agree that you could almost see C. A. Doxiadis slowly unfold the city on land the way he might have done with drawings on a desk: roads rolled out, house foundations dug, markets erected, trees planted. As we looked down from the Margalla Hills, where Naeem rode on the back of his friends' motorcycles and

I stood at Viewpoint with my parents, we didn't imagine Alexander the Great and Genghis Khan riding their armies on the Pothohar Plateau, on the edge of which the city was emerging. But, always, on a clear day and in the space of a few minutes on an airplane lifting away from the city, it was possible to see how small the sliver of ground beneath our feet was: in a miracle of nature, the Margalla Hills become the Murree Hills become the Himalayas, and the Pothohar Plateau, hundreds of miles wide, trickled down to nothing, like us.

•

My mother, white and taller than my father by a few inches, did not stand out in Islamabad as much as you would think. For one thing, the capital was sparsely populated so there weren't many people to compare her against. ("Where are all the *people?*" my grandfather used to say to my father. "Not here, because they have more sense than you!") And where there were others, they, too, were foreigners, employees at embassies or any of the network of international organizations that existed even then.

There was a time in that first year that I recall her completely out of place, but I did not imagine the same of myself or my siblings. A few weeks after we arrived, my aunt took us to the butcher in order to give my mother a lesson on how to buy meat in Pakistan. We piled into her car, our three cousins along with Ayesha and me, all squeezed together in the back seat and in each other's laps. The butcher was like nothing we'd ever seen, although we looked away and pretended otherwise. My mother did not look away and she did not pretend. The "butcher" was an open-aired meat market where carcasses buzzing with flies were impaled with hooks that hung from the meat stalls, dozens of chickens were crowded in stacked cages, and blood flowed in the open drains. My aunt expertly navigated the drains and the stalls, giving instructions regarding her order in one place and taking it to another to be ground or cut as she wanted. My mother walked alongside her, appearing attentive to what she was told, skipping with care over the drains and swatting at the flies, all the while intending never to return.

When the outing was complete and we returned to my aunt's, my mother instructed us to take off our shoes at the door. She reappeared with a rag, dropped to her bare knees, and scrubbed clean the soles of our shoes, all while my aunt cried, "Leave it, leave it! I'll get someone else to do it," and my mother paid her no mind and embarrassed us all.

"We can do without meat," I'd overhear her say when my father returned from work. But that wasn't necessary because not too long after that, a butcher of the type she was accustomed to opened a shop a few streets away in Kohsar market. That butcher's well-stocked deep freezers and glass display cases guaranteed that she would find ground beef, chicken breasts, cuts of lamb, and anything else she fancied.

The day we moved from our aunt's home into our own, two servants met us at the driveway, both in white uniforms my aunt had tailored for them. My mother looked at my father and at them as we emptied the car, wondering who they were. When my father said they were our employees, she looked taken aback and said she did not need help. They followed us into the house, prising bags from our hands, and soon served tea to my parents on trays. There were a few heated conversations between my parents over the next few days, but my mother would not budge. She said she did not want to worry about the proximity of young men she couldn't trust to her daughters. My father shook his head and tried to convince her otherwise.

"This is a big house," he said, as if she hadn't noticed that it was larger than the house he'd built in which tenants would live for decades. "Who will do everything?"

"What? You don't think I can?" she challenged him.

The designated cook made a batch of cinnamon rolls that rivaled those served to us at a new American friend's home, but the servants were gone by the end of the month. From then on, my mother cooked, cleaned, polished, prepared, and did anything else that making the house hers required.

"Have mercy!" she would shout when we left a room without bothering to pick up our mess. But still angry at leaving Vienna, we had little mercy for her in those days.

While she could do without help at home, and without our endlessly delayed moving shipment that included boxes of her favorite books, she decided she could no longer do without paintings. My parents had two or three small paintings by Pakistani artists that had been gifted to them over the years in Vienna, which were now dwarfed on the walls of our Islamabad living room, an area twice the size of the one we'd left behind. At that time, I knew of only one painting from her childhood, a postcard-size portrait by a student of a Dutch painter that had hung for years above her grandmother's bed. I had not yet seen the family photograph taken the night before she boarded a ship to Chicago when she was eighteen. In that grainy black and white image I will find, the bottom third of a gargantuan painting is visible behind her.

A few months after our arrival, without giving anyone notice, Thera buys a painting. She is wearing her favorite dress, a batik that is all shades of brown with a trail of square buttons she will save when the fabric is worn through. She drives alone from Islamabad to Rawalpindi, where there is an exhibit of Pakistani painters in the Art Galleries. The name is generous, because in the Civil Lines neighborhood, which was built by the British in the garrison town, the Art Galleries looks like a house. I picture her in the presence of the painting for the first time, the moment she makes the decision to buy the unexpected artwork.

She observes it from a distance and, quickly, stands within reach. I imagine her overwhelmed with a desire to sink into the kaleidoscope of luminous color the way she must have dreamed, in those early years, of plunging into my father's world. From the moment she sees it, she believes it is what it is not: a calligraphic rendering of the shahada. She, like all converts, recited the shahada when she became Muslim and married my father. *There is no God but Allah and Mohammed is his messenger,* the principal tenet of Islam holds. She is compelled to buy a painting by an unfamiliar artist without consulting my father. She is still wearing the dress when my father returns late from the office and she claps her hands together and tells him what she has done. He looks at her worriedly when she says she spent the household money on it, but when it arrives the next day, he receives it with delight and her joy doubles.

When the painting is hung, it is like nothing else in our home. The entirety is a wild palette of color, full of what the artist's son will one day describe to me as Indian yellow and olive green, and my favorite, cobalt blue. Texture unfurls throughout, as if a brush has rested too long pulling paint and a child's hand has pressed wooden stamps into wet paint. It is modern, I remember thinking, and nothing like us.

Afterwards, whenever my mother was asked about the painting that lit up our living room, she'd repeat the shahada.

"*La ilaha illallah.* . . . Don't you see it?" she would say to a guest, jumping up to stand beside it and sweeping her arms alongside the dance of bold brush strokes.

My father, ever patient with her exuberance, saw it as well. "Here," he'd say, and slowly rise from his chair to point to where it began.

The three of us would roll our eyes at what became a well-rehearsed skit, although not at any moment did we imagine that the painting was anything but the shahada.

•

Islamabad had its ghosts, but so did we. While my father had parents, siblings, and more cousins than we could count, my mother only had the family that she'd left. Her family consisted of her sister who'd moved to New York and with whom my mother stayed close, a brother with whom she communicated perhaps once a year, a mother who'd died when my brother was six months old, and a father who'd died long ago in an unspecified war. The fact that my mother never spoke of her father (or the war) settled him into death more easily.

One afternoon when I was in high school, a one-page letter arrived for her from Amsterdam. In the official letter signed and stamped by a notary was her father's name. We found her at the kitchen table, the envelope in her hand. Her eyes were red and they stayed that way for days. She left the letter on the kitchen table, where she'd opened it, as if picking it up again was a burden heavier than she could bear. We tried to imagine a loss so large it could account for her sorrow, but we could not. Eventually, she told us the truth. Her father had died. Of course she'd known her father was alive, but he'd been as good as dead to her. Twenty years earlier, when she was young and lived in Amsterdam, he'd disowned her, along with her brother and sister, when he deserted his dying wife for a longtime mistress and, eventually, a new apartment a short walk away on Beethovenstraat.

With her palm open on the letter on the kitchen table, my mother said, "My father was dead to me for a long time. Now he is dead to the world." Her eyes were still red, rawer than the voice in which she added, "Nothing has changed."

We sat with her, full of questions we could not articulate. Eventually, my mother returned the letter to the envelope. She studied us as if she had something more to say.

"You've seen him," she said to me.

"What?"

"Remember?" she said, and reminded me of a holiday in Amsterdam when I was six. In the city center, on a busy street, we'd waited at a traffic light.

"You want me to remember a traffic light?" I asked.

She said we'd all been in the car, my father behind the wheel waiting for the red light to change. An older man in a hat and overcoat walked in the crosswalk in front of us and she yelped at the sight of him.

"You thought Daddy had hit someone," she said.

I remembered. She'd cried out and I'd jumped and hit my head.

"That was him."

It was a while before I spoke. "What was his name?"

"Why?" she answered, but then she gave it to me. "Leo."

"Leo," I say for the first time, the name of a grandfather I did not know was alive until he was dead.

"You remember my mother's name?" she added, but I didn't answer. My mother slipped her mother's middle name, Yolanda, into mine, so I cannot help but take *Eleonora* with me and keep her close.

Later that night, when my father returned from the office and I said goodnight to my parents, my mother offered another detail. She and Leo had last spoken when she was twenty-two and she needed his permission to marry my father because Holland's Napoleonic law still required it. To her surprise, he took her telephone call. But he declined to give his consent until she threatened to publicize his refusal with a classified ad in the newspaper, and when he arrived in the city office to record permission, a clerk called her to confirm his identity. In the background of the call, she heard her father insist he had no children, not even one, but he finally signed the form.

"There was a document like that in those days?" I asked.

"Napoleonic laws required all sorts of documents."

"What was it called?" I asked, not sure I believed her.

"What do you care?" she snapped before adding, "Extract of something." But that night, the story that had begun with Leo and now included Napoleon sounded more like a fairy tale than my mother's life, so I didn't think about it further.

•

A few years later, I experienced my first real death and it belonged to a whole country.

I was seventeen when Pakistan's Prime Minister Zulfikar Ali Bhutto was hanged early one morning. A noose was tied around his neck and he said, "Finish it!" and a trap door fell underneath him and his hangman declared him dead. He was buried without his wife or children, settled into the ground before prayers could be offered and final (or is it first?) goodbyes were said.

I remember my father, his face gray like my hair is now, and my mother tall and white as ever in a zippered bathrobe, a strand of fine hair caught in her mouth. Each went about the early morning charting distinct rhythms for their grief. I was awoken by the racket of my mother putting away the previous night's dishes. Then, from my window, I watched my father, lost in his thoughts and oversized pajamas, walk the garden and pace the driveway, before he saw our chowkidar, and the two reached for each other as if they were old friends. I heard a stifled sob, at least one, which might have been my father's, even though the only time I'd seen him cry was when his brother died, we still lived in Vienna, and the death of a prime minister, at least that one, wouldn't have mattered to me. I turned away from the window.

As a rule, death happened to other people. But on the morning of April 4, 1979, my world tilted and my stomach lurched. Death had a taste, iron like blood and jasmine like flowers, and it was in my mouth when I joined my parents for breakfast. It would taste the same again thirty-seven years later when I leaned over my mother's body in the morgue.

The radio blasted more static than words in the kitchen, but my mother turned up the volume. It had been seven years since my father had moved us to Pakistan and his country changed everything about me. It had even changed the color of my skin; I hadn't noticed, but overnight, and in all the ways that mattered to me, it had become decidedly brown.

My mother poured my father's second cup of tea and added toast to the basket near him. Her hand grazed his as she sat down, and she kept it there, their knuckles touching for a few moments more.

"Eat," my mother instructed me.

"I'm not going to school today," I said.

The International School of Islamabad was a misnomer, as it was mostly American, and my classmates were the children of CIA agents or US embassy personnel or USAID workers or ARAMCO employees.

"You will be on the bus, end of story," my father said.

"Why?"

"You will not give anyone the satisfaction of knowing you don't want to be there."

"What?"

"After what the Americans have done . . . ," my father said, leaving what they'd done hanging over breakfast like it would hang over the country. "You will get on the bus and take your sister."

I knew better than to hesitate, so I finished my eggs, and as I put my lunch in my bag, my mother said her piece.

"I will not live here under that criminal," she said, because no one in our family needed the name of the criminal, the general who'd overthrown the prime minister with US assent and effectively sentenced him to death. "Living under the Germans was one thing. Living under a murderer is another."

"The Germans weren't murderers?" my father said, getting up and pushing his chair back with his legs, his patience all gone.

"You know precisely what I mean," my mother muttered as he left.

Bhutto's son, Shahnawaz, had graduated from our school by then, as had Omar. Begum Bhutto, the prime minister's wife, spoke at their graduation, glamorous in a sari, my mother equally regal in her own. Shah, as we called him, was young and handsome, and years earlier when I thought myself still a child, he'd picked me up and tossed me in the air, my pigtails slapping his face. "I'm going to marry you one day," he joked, and I giggled. I thought of Shah on the bus ride the morning we heard the news, what it meant for your father to go from the breakfast table to a hastily dug grave, with a two-year jail stay in between, time enough, I knew, to write *If I am Assassinated* and for abscesses the size of golf balls to rot his jaws.

Bhutto's death would haunt me for years afterwards. I carried it with me like a secret to my small college in a corner of Pennsylvania because there no one seemed to know anything at all about Pakistan or the dead prime minister, and this made the magnitude of the death more curious. How could Pakistan be a subject of a country's surveillance yet invisible to its citizens? Now, when I look back upon it, I imagine the death propelled me to graduate school where I tried to make sense of what 1979 meant to the world. Over time, the sounds of a body falling and a neck snapping, alive in my imagination as if I'd been in the dank room, slowly receded as details often do. When I became a mother, I remembered it again. The date, April 3, meant nothing when I went into labor, but the next day, flush with hormones and new life a day old, and with my father holding Kamal in his arms and the April 4th *New York Times* perched on the windowsill, I remembered, grateful for the day that separated my baby from that death anniversary.

•

I have no memory of speaking to my parents about race—mine—when I was a child. I did not think to lay my arm next to theirs and compare skin color because the difference was obvious and sometimes facts don't merit discussion. *The sun rises, night falls, our colors differ.* When our differences were a topic of conversation, they were situated in place.

"You have the best of both worlds," my father would always say, as if Pakistan were its own world, which it was.

"The world you live in! You children don't know how lucky you have it," my mother would say, as if luck were a place that forever separated us. We had a father who loved us, a mother who was alive, food on the table (and in the refrigerator), and above all, we'd been spared war. "You really lack for nothing," she'd sometimes marvel.

In my senior year of high school, when it came time to fill out college applications, I needed a category that described what I was, and asked, "Mummy, what am I?"

"What does it *matter?*" my mother responded, when she looked up from *Ragtime* or *Shogun* or whatever she was reading then. When I sat next to her waving an application, she said, "Mixed, of course," and that was that.

Only there was no such category on the form. Neither was there a slot for Pakistani Dutch or Dutch Pakistani, so I gravitated to "Other," which is where I still live.

When my father returned from the office, he suggested I select "Caucasian" because Pakistan, or Pakistani Dutch, was not a race and, strictly speaking, that's what we were.

"Daddy! I'm not white!"

"But you're Other?" he asked, genuinely amused.

"What's wrong with that?" I asked.

I had never given color much thought as a child in Vienna, but the International School of Islamabad changed all that. Sometimes, color is acquired when difference is made obvious and the reality of what that means (you are less valuable) sets in.

"Why, there's nothing wrong with that!"

"I'm brown, you know," I explained to my father, the brownest of us all, whose category was also not listed on my college application.

"Of course you are, darling," my father said, kissing my forehead.

A few days before I left for college, my father took me on a long drive through Islamabad's streets, which meant we ended up traversing the city more than once. He gave me tips on how to find a job (quickly), instructions on how to manage my money (carefully), and told me to write to my mother often (weekly). He repeated his mantra regarding education. "No one will ever be able to take it away from you. Study hard." I was only half listening, because he hadn't said anything he hadn't already said before. Until he did.

"One more thing," he said, when we turned into our street.

"Yes?" I said, waiting.

"This one thing," he said and paused again. When he finally spoke, he cautioned me not to "come home" with a Black or Jewish husband.

"Why?" I remember asking the brown man who'd married white.

"Too difficult," he whispered.

Then we were home where my mother waited for us.

FOUR

Naeem and I met again in 1983, almost a dozen years after our time in Islamabad overlapped. We were both in Denver, a city almost exactly on the other side of the world from Islamabad and along another mountain range. We were both pursuing international studies in graduate school, he was completing a PhD, and I was beginning the master's program. I spotted his smile from across our graduate school lounge. In the space of a few minutes, we figured out what was true. He'd played soccer with Omar, I'd sat next to his brother in sixth grade, and our parents' homes were a few miles apart, both along Margalla Road. Not long after, we pedaled side by side on bicycles in the Rockies, sometimes with his hand on my lower back to help me up the steepest climbs. Ayesha visited and we took her cross-country skiing, and when she got so cold she couldn't move, he put her feet in his armpits to warm them. He packed his wok and knives and spices into an oversized backpack with an aluminum frame and rode his red bicycle to my place to cook elaborate meals for my roommates and me. Eventually, we packed our laundry into his mountain climbing backpack and walked ten minutes across a small park to a laundromat on Evans to do it together.

By the time Naeem and I decided to marry, my parents had heard about his brother who had been diagnosed with schizophrenia. My father worried about the health of his grandchildren and my mother suggested we needn't have them. I ignored them both. At twenty-three, I was young, healthy, and in love, and the possibility of anything going wrong in our lives, much less with hypothetical children, was too remote to bear consideration. But then I mentioned the name of Naeem's father's village, Bavra Kona, which my father believed translated from Punjabi to English as *Mad Corner*. My father slapped his forehead and asked me to consult a doctor about the genetics of mental illness. A few days later, a doctor listened to scraps of family history that I'd gleaned from Naeem before predicting (like a weather forecast) that as long as Naeem was not a schizophrenic, our children wouldn't be either. My mother said, "Well, I certainly hope he's right," as if she was certain he wasn't, and my father said, "Alright then," and kept future worries to himself. After we married, my father and I shared a running joke.

"Don't blame me for marrying into a crazy family," he would say, holding back a giggle.

"Even though you let me?" I'd respond, while we both dissolved into laughter and my mother looked away.

•

Naeem's teaching job took us to Syracuse, New York, where after three moves in thirteen months, we finally arrived at our new one-bedroom apartment in a repurposed school in Solvay. I wasn't interested then, but the village on the southwest edge of Onondaga Lake owes its name to the Solvay Process, imported by a Belgian, Ernest Solvay, in the late 1800s. The industrial process uses salt brine, limestone, and ammonia to produce soda ash, necessary for glass and present in detergent, fabric dyes, and much more. The company, absorbed by Allied Chemical Corporation, devastated Onondaga Lake, turning what was sacred to the native Onondaga people into a horribly polluted body of water.

We arrived a year after the Solvay Process Plant closed and left behind the wreckage of economic loss. But for us, transplants connected to Syracuse University rather than the area, we hardly noticed. As we carried boxes into our apartment, a passerby told us that she'd been unable to hang her laundry out to dry because of soot from the plant. I imagined her laundry line each time the wind shifted off the lake and brought a sharp odor that embarrassed me in the company of friends. As far as we were concerned, Solvay and Syracuse were the same, both victims of the collapse of the industrial Steel Belt. Abandoned or razed buildings were scattered along the way from downtown Syracuse to Solvay, regardless of which route you took. There were few restaurants in Syracuse that offered ethnic cuisines: Italian (when we arrived), Thai (after our first child was born), King David's (still there) on the university strip, and a single quasi-Mexican restaurant (long gone) known for fat squares of chocolate cake. Syracuse was a far cry from Denver, new and sunlit for three hundred days. When our moving shipment arrived from Denver and we were counting out the extra charge required by two flights of stairs, the truck driver laughed at our landing spot. "Look around. Shouldn't we all be moving west?" he quipped.

In Solvay, at my writing desk, Lahore moved into me. While Naeem taught, I ate on my grandparents' latticed verandah and sat on the ground next to my grandmother in the outdoor kitchen of 5 Queen's Road, listening to the pop of mustard seeds and the sizzle of onions in the black frying pan. One of my characters died as I sat on the landing of our building, below a huge window beyond which lay the poisoned lake. I remember the stab of sun on my right cheek, the sharpened No. 2 pencil in my hand, the old clipboard against my knees, an acrid breeze when the door to the outside opened and Naeem came home. I dreamed of Lahore that night, Onondaga Lake the backdrop to the buckled stone patio of my grandparents' home where my character died all over again and his funeral pyre was being built. Even then, it was possible to imagine I became a writer because of 5 Queen's Road. More than subject matter, the house gave me my bearings, the way my parents did, coordinates on a map for what (and where) was possible. In my grandparents' home, time was elastic, like it is in a novel. The past and present existed simultaneously, and sometimes, like being lost on the page, my footing was wobbly.

Our building in Solvay stood next to Prospect Firehouse, a working fire station that sounded an eight o'clock siren as if to alert workers to their morning shifts. For the most part, though, we were oblivious to details that would have illuminated our nearness to the plant and its history. A tramway in the sky had once run a few blocks from our door: an aerial cable road fitted with buckets the size of pianos and spaced eighty feet apart carried crushed limestone a few miles from Split Rock's quarries to the Solvay plant. Deep in the ground, pipes of salt water had once flowed from wells in Tully twenty-two miles away to the Solvay plant. And at the corner of Milton and Willis Avenues, on a hill we didn't notice and on a short walk we never took, a five-million-gallon reservoir had once stored the brine. All this had passed away—taken apart, carried away, or buried in the invisible graveyard of the past.

•

I can summon the sounds of that Syracuse day as if they made a favorite piece of music, but the melody brings dread, not joy. A gush of water fills our acrylic bathtub. Naeem's moans match the slip of oil on skin as I massage his back. The telephone receiver drop-clicks in the wall mount. The bathroom door catches and stops as he uses the bathroom again and again. The soundscape survives and so, too, does the cast of details it unleashes. I have a precise memory of a single thought: this man who is my husband and works almost every hour of each day cannot find it in him to return home on time from a Sunday morning at the gym. Our living room is extraordinarily bright and the shafts of swirling dust buzz. The ceiling-high bookcase appears to have fallen into the glass tabletop where colorful novels rise in stacks.

Naeem is wearing black shorts, a signature bandana (likely red), a gym towel (not ours) draped around his neck. His face is ash gray, an unnatural version of itself. When he lies facedown on the living room floor, one side of his half-open mouth is distended against the carpeting. His smooth back, always beautiful, is surprisingly salty when I kiss it.

Strange, then, that the night which followed is mute. This, despite the fact that I spent it at a Ravi Shankar concert ninety miles away in Rochester. I went without Naeem, though he had a ticket too, because we were loath to let our tickets go to waste. Perhaps that's why my mind erased it—because I feel I shouldn't have gone, that I shouldn't have enjoyed a note. I cannot recollect the simplest detail of the sitar maestro, whether there was more than one performer, where our friend Laura and I sat in relation to the stage, or if there was an intermission. But it seems important, this music that I went to hear while, without my knowledge, my husband's heart was dying.

On the off chance that a recording was made, and that it still exists twenty-seven years after the fact, I write the Eastman School of Music. I provide the only two details I've retained: the date and location of the concert. I immediately receive a scanned copy of the concert program. I stare at the first page of the email attachment. By my calculation, the concert's seven-thirty start time on the evening of April 29, 1990, is approximately ten hours after Naeem had a heart attack on a treadmill in a gym near the YMCA in Syracuse. I know now, but didn't know then, that the concert and my long, pleasant drive to Rochester with our friend (*We mustn't waste the tickets! Go on,* Naeem told me) fell within the twelve-hour window in which patients who do not receive medical treatment for cardiac arrest usually die. To my surprise, a concert recording exists and, if I'm patient, it can be digitized, and I can listen to it in the Eastman library.

It takes almost six months for the recording to become available, but the day finally arrives when I again drive alone to

Rochester. It's late September and uncannily like that unseasonably bright and warm day in April. The central New York sky is uncommonly clear, the only clouds trailing wisps produced by aircraft. Rich farmland rolls toward Cayuga Lake east of Route 96 and Seneca Lake on the west, all of it being put to sleep by farmers in anticipation of winter. On the thruway, trees rush by my windows like a moving painting, but it's early autumn and the tips are brushed with golds, reds, and yellows, as if an artist changed her mind at the last moment and added bursts of color at the top of every tree. I'm reminded of my pregnancies' hallucinatory dreams, in which magnificent liquid colors bled in and out of each other in a luminosity I haven't seen since.

On the recording, Ravi Shankar introduces the first piece, and his Indian accent, so similar to a Pakistani accent, comforts me. The raag's opening, the alap, is a dialog between the musician and the raag that sets the scene, much like opening paragraphs in a novel. I'm in downtown Rochester, in the listening room of Sibley Music Library, surrounded by cubicles like the one I'm sitting in, outfitted with complex audio equipment. I'm sitting on the floor, almost under the desk with the sound system into which I've inserted the CD, and I stay there for the alap and everything that follows in Raag Puriya Kalyan, momentarily transfixed by an overwhelming pathos of classical Indian music. When the tabla and sitars are in full thrall, they pull each other through terrific crescendos and explosive trills. *How could I have forgotten this?* I wonder. Later, the audience roars, and I realize I'd forgotten that as well, though it must have moved me to have shared the moment of reverence. I only realize that I'm swaying back and forth with the music when someone comes to my corner of the listening room to look disapprovingly at my squeaking chair. When Laura shares her memory of the concert with me, she recalls only the tabla. She thinks this is because the concert was her introduction to the instrument, but after listening to the recording, I tell her it's because of the solos.

The forgiving afternoon light means the drive home is more beautiful than the drive to Rochester, but I'm preoccupied by something else: the story I've just discovered about Ravi Shankar's son, Shubho, who was also playing that night. Ravi Shankar died in his nineties some years ago, but his son, Shubho Shankar, is also dead, at fifty, from a protracted illness and pneumonia, and, it seems to me, from heartbreak. After giving up his sitar, he'd returned to it in his forties, left California for India to study with his mother (after a twenty-year absence during which they'd been estranged), and eventually enjoyed a resurgence in his career, which included touring again with his father. In December of the same year we saw him, he played an Indian festival where critics claimed he played off-key. Recordings show this wasn't the case, but he was inconsolable. He declared it too late in life to continue musical training, left India and his mother, gave up the sitar, and was dead less than two years later.

My memory of that evening is unaltered by what I hear—there is no music, no sound. When I returned from the concert, Naeem was much the same as when I'd left, perhaps worse. In my absence, he'd been instructed over the telephone by an emergency room physician to take Imodium, drink fluids, and sleep. For the rest of the night, he paced, visited the bathroom, and tossed in bed. All the while, he behaved like a complete stranger, one overcome by what he described as a crushing yet non-specific sense of dread. At the time, his amplified anxiety, terror even, seemed melodramatic. *Who was this person I married? Is this how he intended to behave when life threw him viruses that gave him diarrhea and made him vomit?* Perhaps we slept some that night, but what I recall is that Naeem's sweat drenched the bed and made me cold.

During a doctor's appointment the next day, Naeem was diagnosed with a viral illness and told to rest, which made us certain he was hardly sick at all. A week passed, and still, Naeem could hardly climb the stairs of the Maxwell School of Citizenship and Public Affairs at the university where classes had ended and final exams had begun. He ascended the four flights excruciatingly slowly, pausing at each landing before using the bannister to climb the next set of stairs. At the top, he allowed himself a longer rest by sinking into a secretary's chair until his heart stopped racing and he was able to walk the remaining hundred yards to his office. He complained about his vision, episodes in which a dark shadow zigzagged, floating from the periphery to the center, followed by sharp headaches that lasted hours. The symptoms and trips to the doctor persisted for a month that included a Memorial Day picnic at Jamesville Reservoir and a softball game with friends from my writing workshop. Naeem labored for breath as we set up the diamond and was picked last for teams. I groaned with everyone else when he hobbled toward first base, an easy out.

Naeem was thirty-three the night I went to the concert. He was thirty-four a month later at his fourth doctor's appointment, the only time I accompanied him. He was seeing Dr. Chen again, the man who had been insisting for weeks that it was just a virus. I was startled to hear my name called in the busy waiting room, and I joined Naeem just as he was being helped from the examining table. Dr. Chen was hunched over pages of EKG graphs, fine-point pen outlines of delicate mountain peaks and plunging cliffs on red squares of graph paper. Dr. Chen was a slight man, more so when he sat and his white doctor's coat billowed. But he was like us, a foreigner in Syracuse, New York, and without wanting to, we felt sorry for him. "The patient knows best," he remarked, shaking his head. What did he mean? Fear hadn't taken hold yet. Naeem was taciturn, as he is in moments of crisis.

"What do you recommend?" he finally asked, as if our sympathy as fellow foreigners meant we could still trust him.

"You've likely had a heart attack," Dr. Chen said. "You must see a cardiologist."

"When?"

"Now."

I ran a red light on W. Genesee an hour later (and a month too late) on the way to the cardiologist's office.

"Are you trying to kill us?" Naeem asked sensibly, "Because I'd like to live."

The imaging room was far too small and crowded with medical professionals, but I stayed anyway. After a fluster of activity, the technician glided her ultrasound wand over his shaved chest. The bulky machine produced a grainy picture that silenced everyone. The cardiologist leaned forward and tapped his fingernails against the screen while he drew an outline around the damaged heart muscle that filled it.

"Cocaine," he said confidently.

"No," Naeem said. There was no drug usage, nor was there a family history of cardiac disease. Naeem was young and in good health. There was absolutely no explanation for what the cardiologist proclaimed to be a major heart attack.

"A few days ago, I saw a patient with a heart attack like yours," he said. "She'd been in an argument with her husband at the time." And then he paused as if we, too, might reveal such circumstances.

The steady *whoosh*-ing of Naeem's heartbeat should have reassured me that he was all right now, but it did not. I knew what I had seen. Captured by the wand, lying at the cardiologist's fingertips, present in black and grays, shifting shape ever so slightly with each pulse, was the shadow of death. The cardiologist looked at me for the first time.

"He's not dead," he said.

We took Erie Boulevard home, slicing through the Steel Belt city on what had been an artery of the Erie Canal. The late afternoon was a familiar gray; this time the color suffocated like a fog, as if the shadow on the screen had followed us outside, slipped into our car, and was accompanying us home.

I called my parents with the news.

My mother was speechless.

My father asked, "Do you want me to come?"

"Now?" I quickly replied, as if my father's offer might disappear.

"Heart attack?" my mother asked before we said goodbye. "Are you sure?"

When my father arrived from Pakistan the following month, and stayed almost a week, I realized that I'd never in my whole life spent that much time alone with him. We sat in the living room of our Solvay apartment and watched Wimbledon for hours each day. Martina Navratilova won and won, and Stefan Edberg beat Boris Becker in a five-set match. For that week, things were as they should be. Wimbledon had been part of my childhood, a family pastime no matter where we were in the world. One summer weekend in 1975, we'd escaped to Murree and instead of hiking, we spent it listening to the voices of British radio announcers compete with static on my father's shortwave. Arthur Ashe beat Jimmy Connors for the championship and my parents, walking the radio from corner to corner of the room in search of better reception, whooped with joy. Arthur Ashe was Black, my mother was white, my father was brown, and no one needed to explain the joy of the moment to my siblings and me.

That winter, when Naeem's resting heart rate was thirty, only a few beats less than his age, we flew home to be with our parents. There, in Islamabad, my father suggested Naeem see a cardiologist, as if a Pakistani might have better luck bringing his heart muscle back to life. Naeem underwent a thallium stress test to assess the damage. After being injected with the radioisotope and riding a stationary bike, Naeem waited.

The young doctor tried to be gentle in the face of discouraging films, but by then the diagnosis was old. Eventually, we discussed Denver and the Rocky Mountains, and in an aside, he instructed Naeem not to run in airports, which I recall each time we're in one. Finally, he asked, "Do you have children?"

"Not yet," I answered, to which he looked at both of us and softly replied, "It would be the best thing for you."

I might have been embarrassed at the intrusion, but there was nothing more intimate than watching Naeem's saggy heart pump slowly on the screen and hearing the doctor describe it as dead.

Years later, when I tell Ayesha about this conversation while we eat carrot cake in a London restaurant, she will laugh so hard the waiter brings us extra water to make her stop. "In Pakistan," she finally says with tears streaming down her face, "there's absolutely nothing that a marriage or baby can't fix."

•

We brought both our children home to Solvay. Natalie Cole brought her father back to life in his songs as we drove to the hospital when I was in labor with Kamal. For years, I'd remember the sound of her voice on Erie Boulevard as we passed the Art Deco building that dominates that side of the city with its stainless steel figure perched high like a new age helmeted angel overlooking us all. I don't know what music played on the way back from the hospital, but I remember that Naeem stopped at a southwest corner where Syracuse becomes Solvay to show off our baby to Rick, our car mechanic. Nusrat Fateh Ali Khan's *Mustt Mustt* and the Gipsy Kings' *Allegria* were two sides of the cassette in my Walkman the morning after Shahid was born and the doctor walked into my hospital room and joked at the sleeping baby in my arms, "Haven't we seen this one before?" Naeem never had much patience for comparisons. "They are themselves," he would say. But he had even less patience when he was the source of comparisons, which he often was. *He has the shape of your head! Your lips! Your eyes!* His frustration was always the same. "Who cares who they look like, as long as they have your heart."

Everything is more pressing when you have children, including grasping exactly where you're standing, a fact that Naeem, at least, almost always knows. On our first visit to Pakistan after Kamal was born, we used the money from the publication of my first story to take PIA's two-hour airplane safari to see our exact coordinates from the air for ourselves. The plane flew over Pakistan's northern areas, famed places one or both of us had visited with our parents, always by road: Hunza, Gilgit, Chitral, Swat, Naran. We flew along the Karakoram to the Hindu Kush range while the pilot recited what lay below: some of the highest glaciers outside of the Arctic circle and Baltora, one of the longest; the world's great mountains, like K-2, Nanga Parbat, and also Rakaposhi, which became one of Naeem's most amusing nicknames for Kamal, who did not even reach his waist. Soon, PIA's air safaris were discontinued and the city we knew had leaked out of its squares across multiple lanes of Margalla Road into sectors I couldn't identify and in areas marked as nature preserves on C. A. Doxiadis's blueprints. But by then, I'd begun preserving our Islamabad on the page, replete with white and blue rectangular concrete street signs that sat on every corner, flaking red paint of metal monkey bars in empty parks, and stairs that led nowhere in abandoned, half-constructed houses. The Islamabad of our childhood was the map of my stories.

I discovered Solvay's own deep and complicated history late, twenty years after we left. Finding it was like laying a transparency on an overhead projection of my memories—a map over a map. Saint Cecilia's, used by Irish Catholics, was built on land donated by the Solvay Process Plant. It is the church on Woods Road in which my mother-in-law, visiting after Kamal was born, wandered in to convince a priest that his god was the same as hers. Jerome's Hill was carved with a tunnel to allow a cable tramway easier passage from the quarry to the plant. It is

the unnamed hill I skirted when I pushed Kamal in his red jog-
ging stroller on walks around the neighborhood. Lamont Avenue housed the Tyrol Club, built for Tyrolians in 1944, and is
the site of a high school graduation party we once attended. The
intersection of Hall and Milton was the end of the cable line
and home to a stone pile which divided East and West Solvay.
It is the parking lot at the bottom of a street of houses that are
forlorn compared to the splendid ones (rumored to have heated
driveways) west on Orchard Road. Solvay's grand library was
funded by Andrew Carnegie, but also Frederick Hazard, the son
of the Solvay plant's founder. It is the place I most frequented,
even more than the elementary school playground after Kamal
was born. No one knows why, but Hazard school contained
four frieze panels that were plaster-cast reproductions of marble
sculptures in Florence Cathedral made by Luca della Robbia. On
the street by the same name with its own fire station is the park
where Kamal collected acorns. The two-bedroom one-bath red
house on Woods Road was built in 1895 and lost half its value
in foreclosure some years ago. It is what I saw if I leaned just so
from my desk near the window, like the day the police entered
the kitchen of the red house at lunchtime after the son, a high
school student, put a gun to his head in front of his parents and
killed himself.

Eventually, we would leave Solvay, just as we'd left Islamabad. A few days before moving, and all at once, dog-day cicadas emerged from their slumber in the wooded hill across our
street. True to their name, it happened in the dog days of July
or August when Sirius in the Canis Major constellation is bright
in the sky. After spending up to five years in the earth, the cicadas burrowed their way out, climbed to the top of the trees, and
cast off their skin to fly. Their mating song was a buzz saw gone
wrong, an earsplitting version of crickets at a specious pitch and
time of day. I closed the windows but they failed to keep out the
racket and transformed our apartment into a baking oven, so

that rivulets of perspiration dripped down my back. I was transported to my first summer in Islamabad, when my parents satisfied my childhood pleas and erected a tent in our bare back lawn, complete with a tiny irrigation ditch to catch the monsoon rain that turned the ground into mud. The canvas tent swarmed with mosquitos, despite being sprayed with DDT, and was never raised again. Leaning over to pick up more books and add them to a tomato box salvaged for our move from a grocery store, I remembered the smell of the earthworms and cockroaches in that summer's mud.

Our baby cried and cried and cried, and I wanted my mother. Shahid never slept, not at night and not during the day and not after his pediatrician berated me for the expectation. Exhausted, I'd put him in his crib while I packed. Several boxes later, my resolve broke. I sprinted the few steps to our wall of windows and threw open every single one, standing in the path of the cicada noise on which, I swear, a gentle breeze rode in. The cacophony of Shahid's cries and the cicadas' drone almost felled me. I opened the bedroom door where our round baby, wearing only a diaper in his crib, had pulled himself up and stopped crying. I reached for him, his soft brown skin red with heat and slippery with sweat and tears, his baby heart pounding hard against me as I buried kisses in his triple chin. When his father came home, the apartment smelled of dusk and life, and he and Kamal lay on the floor and blew raspberries on Shahid's belly, their smiles one. A bus strained up the street, past the red house and library, and it drowned out the cicadas before it got to the church. The boys, deaf to all the noise but theirs, laughed in unison.

We take our cities with us, I thought, and I wondered what our children's would be.

FIVE

In this memory, my father is sixty-three years old, the age Naeem is now. We are standing in front of the windows that faced the lawn where my parents pitched that tent for me during our first summer in the house. We are alone when he guesses that he has ten years left to live. He makes the comment nonchalantly, as if he'd known it all along and it was hardly worth sharing.

And when he died on schedule ten years later in 1999, just shy of seventy-three, I could recall nothing more about what was said. I can still see his hands deep in his pockets, his gold cashmere sweater bunched over his belt, and the flat light flooding the room as gray as it ever came in Islamabad.

He'd traveled to Vienna from Islamabad for bypass surgery we did not know he needed until my parents called to tell us that it had been scheduled. When he spoke to me for the last time, it was from his hospital bed the night before the surgery. The phone line crackled with static when he asked to speak to the boys because their birthdays, days apart, fell the following week.

"You'll be awake by then!" I shouted.

"Can't. Hear. You."

"You'll—" I said before our connection was interrupted and I waited for the hospital operator to connect us again.

He died in the city of my birth. I was born in Rudolfinerhaus, a small hospital in the 19th district of Vienna, Austria, where a few years later, Ayesha would also be born. The hospital was around the corner from Hofzeile, the street with our post-World War II apartment building yet to fall into disrepair. Directly opposite our short but wide balcony stood a one-time psychiatric hospital, housed in an imperial summer residence built in the 1700s, that was the setting of our childhood nonsense rhyme devised to insult each other. At the corner was the Johannes Nepomuk chapel, named for a patron saint of bridges and protector against floods, which had been absorbed into the Sisters of the Poor Child Jesus Monastery next door. As a child, I was alternately fascinated and terrified by the hospital and chapel. I'd skip by the two buildings wanting nothing more than to enter or flee, sometimes in the same moment.

Twenty-seven years after we'd left Hofzeile for Islamabad, I was overwhelmed with the familiar contradictory impulse. Two days after my siblings and I rushed to Vienna from our corners of the world, the three of us were all leaving again. Charles, Omar's childhood friend and now a doctor, was driving us to Schwechat Airport, and in a few hours, we would abandon Vienna as a family of five for the last time. There, my father's corpse, strapped in a zinc-lined and hermetically sealed coffin, waited to be flown to Lahore where my father would be buried beside his parents. There'd never been any question that my father would be buried in Miani Sahib graveyard, so we'd done what Austrian bureaucracy required and arranged a special coffin and secured a corpse passport. All that remained was to leave.

It was early in the day. We'd begun the journey with my mother and her friend in sight, but we'd lost their car before we left downtown. To our surprise, Charles, a resident of Vienna his whole life, was not embarrassed to say he could best navigate the route from the 19th district, where we'd all once shared Hofzeile. I sensed the narrow street before it arrived, with Rudolfienerhaus set farther off around a wide bend. I closed my eyes and imagined the palace-hospital and chapel-convent. This time, in my thirties and with two children of my own, I willed myself inside the landmarks, their heavy doors flying open just for me, but when the street was a skip away, I wanted to flee them as much as I wanted to flee Vienna.

•

Weeks after my father's death, Naeem and I and our two young sons returned to my parents' already dissolving household in Islamabad so I could begin a pre-planned trip to research my first novel. Although Naeem's parents also lived in Islamabad, we stayed in my parents' home. Eight weeks after we buried him, I walked into my parents' bedroom and opened my father's side of the closet in search of his smell. But his clothes were almost all gone, haphazardly distributed among friends and their sons; ties and suits to one, sweaters to another, an ancient tuxedo worn to a Viennese ball left bundled and alone in a corner until I picked it up. Ayesha and her family lived minutes away on one of Islamabad's two 7th Avenues that lay side by side because one was not enough, and we lamented the lightning-quick dissolution of our home. Neither of us dared complain to my mother, whose life and heart were broken. My father's suits, like the life we'd all known, had disappeared for good.

By then, twenty-eight years had passed since the 1971 war when a Bengali neighbor abandoned his house mid-construction. Yet that rotting, unfinished house of my childhood endured. Squatters lived inside it, and from a distance on a sunny winter day, people, not pants and shirts, appeared draped over bushes to dry. For the first time in my adulthood, I retraced the shortcut from Hill Road to Margalla Road which emptied nearby. The narrow gully cut through a patch of unoccupied land, and young boys chased a ball near a donkey cart with no owner in sight. The children eyed me suspiciously while I went about my grown woman search for initials I'd carved into a tree when I was fifteen and thought I was in love. It had been simple then—a lone young tree in the middle of a secluded path—but now a grove of trees towered over me, and buried in one were my (and his) initials gobbled by layers of bark. Before I was prepared for it, the house appeared and I sprinted all the way home.

I told my mother, but she had no time for my escapade; she only had time for her grief. It was the only thing that was still alive in her, ruling her days and nights and all her future. She did things she could never have imagined, like ridding our home of my father's prized copper collection. He'd spent years accumulating it, searching for antique pieces in the old bazaars of Peshawar, Rawalpindi, Lahore, or wherever he found himself with an hour to spare. Upon learning of my mother's decision, a friend instructed Mohammed, who'd worked for our family since Ayesha and I left home, to hide the copper in a storeroom at the back of our house. In August, he unlocked the door for me, and there on an empty charpai was a pile of copper so heavy the web of rope that was the bed had sunk to the floor.

Naeem and I slept in one of the two bedrooms that faced the Margallas. The desk and wall-length shelves had already been cleared, and all that sat on them was what we'd brought, including the floppy disks that contained early scenes of the novel I was writing. While Naeem slept quickly and peacefully, I'd lie awake and listen to the jackals, and when morning came, to the azaan and a chorus of parrots that arrived with it. Every so often, I'd be struck by the way my cities collided in life and death. The places seemed to move in and out of each other like guests wandering about, looking for a home. My American-born children were asleep in Islamabad in the room next door. My Pakistani father died in Vienna. My Bengali character in the novel I was writing entered the world in New York via a dream that was set in Islamabad. With the memory of my father's body in the belly of an airplane being thrown from one continent to another fresh in my mind, I summoned the dream I'd once had, in which I'd lain on the same mattress, facing the same mountains, confounded by a scene that took place near the foot of the same bed.

In that dream, I awoke to the sound of a girl's soft cries. Behind her, in the wall of windows, the hills were emerging from slumber. Peels of pink slowly lifted the hills into sight. It was spring, and like the jasmine blossoms scenting the air, the girl's "mama" was new. It rolled on her tongue deliciously, as if it had come to her for the first time and she was learning the taste of it. The adolescent girl arrived in pieces: her voice, blue black hair, a slight limp, slanted eyes, small ears glued on a round head. She caught my eye in the mirror and wouldn't let go. She was my daughter.

I didn't have a daughter. At the time of my dream, I was a few months pregnant with our youngest child and as it had been with his brother, I was deep in the short span when vivid dreams and psychedelic colors danced in my head. It was fall and brilliant colors were everywhere in the long New York autumn where leaves held on to color as they did to life. The only way to survive my dream was to write it down and tell no one, not even Naeem, praying that would be enough to keep it from coming true. The girl's name was Noor and she lived in my head and on my pages as if she were real. I gave birth to a healthy son and continued writing my novel, but still today, after all this time, if I'm awake early enough, a dawn arrives and ushers in the moment Noor first appeared. It might be blizzarding in Ithaca, but I'm back in Islamabad, the sun is rising, wood smoke drifts in the open windows, the smooth nap of green carpeting lies on the floor, the corner where the mirror and Noor conspired is alive with the sunrise, and the "mama," crystal clear, is not my sons'.

From then on, I took Noor with me wherever I went, which was why she'd joined us in my parents' home. It was the second time she was there with me, as she'd accompanied me during the short week I was in Islamabad following my father's burial in Lahore. I passed my nights in my sister's old bedroom, where I didn't sleep. Instead, I rummaged through books on the deep shelves which had held my mother's library before they were assembled and alphabetized elsewhere on bookcases built for her.

"How many should we have built for you? One dozen? Two?" my father had teased my mother.

"A room full!" she'd answered, giddy at the thought, and giddy again when they filled half a room.

I looked for, but did not find touchstones of my mother's books, *Tell Me How Long the Train's Been Gone* by James Baldwin or Han Suyin's writings, which had lived in my childhood bedroom. In fact, I didn't recognize any of the titles in Ayesha's room, presumably all acquired since I left home. None of this mattered days after my father's death, because when I opened a book, text bounced on the page the way the world bounced in my mind. So I opened my sister's dresser which I discovered tightly packed with my father's recently organized slide collection. Hundreds of yellow boxes with white labels were scribbled with my mother's loopy handwriting or my father's controlled one, because after living a life together they'd organized it one last time by drawer. I found Dhaka 1971, and with it, imagined Noor. Without telling anyone, I slipped the Bangladesh boxes into my handbag and brought them back to Ithaca.

As I lay beside Naeem and tried to summon the moment Noor arrived in my head, I couldn't remember anything I'd seen on those slides. Had I even looked at them? Later, when I would visit Bangladesh to research my novel and the girl of my dreams, I walked around Dhaka holding up my father's slides to the torrential light, attempting to match his miniature images with what I saw decades later. Like life, the city had changed almost too much to align, except for the boats my father had documented. Back home in Ithaca, I set one of my photographs next to one of his, as if together on my desk, the boats could sail me out of grief.

•

My father had been dead for three or four months and time had taken on a different meaning or none at all. Naeem had returned to his job in Ithaca and my days in Islamabad fell into each other, like the rooms in which they were spent. Mondays were Wednesdays and Thursdays were Sundays and there were books in the kitchen, dinnerware on the landing, carpets on shelves, copper in store rooms. My children, three and seven then, reveled in the disorder, pushing their toys between boxes and dropping them on empty tables. That morning, my mother had caught the boys misbehaving, although I hadn't noticed because everything was amiss. They'd dragged dining room chairs into the living room and laid them upside down as an obstacle course on an imaginary race track for matchbox cars.

"Put them back where they belong," I heard my mother say in a tone that worried me even as an adult. It was clear she hadn't slept well, but perhaps that did not make the difference that morning.

"Why?" Kamal dared. "Are you using them?"

"Play with us, Nani!" Shahid suggested.

"Do as I say."

"No," one said before the other joined in.

"This second!" she shouted and we all jumped.

A short while later, the children were upstairs and not yet fighting, and I went downstairs where I traversed piles of belongings to get to my mother. She was dusting in the lounge, which was the smallest room in the house, had always seen the most use and, for the moment, had been spared disbandment. Even barefoot, as she was then, my mother was taller than me. By 10:30, before the July heat had settled in for the day, she'd tackled most of her morning chores, more devoted to them than ever in the wake of my father's death. She clutched an orange dust cloth, and her brow was damp like the neckline of her cotton house dress.

"Mummy, please don't talk to the boys that way," I said.

"Don't tell me what to do in my house," my mother instantly replied. She bent toward a shelf and prepared to dust a miniature silver tree frame from which tiny faces of her children as children and her grandchildren as they were swung from gnarled limbs.

"It's not right for you to scold them like that," I said weakly and to her back.

My mother dropped the miniature faces to focus on mine. "How dare you speak to me that way."

I laughed, because when I was upset nothing made my mother angrier than if I mocked her.

"Now that your father isn't here, you speak to me like that?"

"He has nothing to do with this, Mother," I said, because she hated to be called *Mother*, he'd been dead for months, and I was right. My voice was raised, but not much because Mohammed was washing dishes in the kitchen and, as if I'd suddenly made him arbiter of my relationship with my mother, I was afraid he was listening.

My mother closed the space between us, her fist lay heavy on my shoulder. I steeled myself for further shouting and waited. In the end, though, I strained to hear her words.

"You children have always been your father's children," she whispered.

She threw the clean dust cloth on the cocktail table, the one my father had hired a carpenter to make so she could be surrounded with the likeness of the Danish furniture she'd loved and left behind in Vienna decades earlier.

"Don't you sit on it," she warned. It was too late because that's where I was, sitting directly in a shaft of sunlight that sliced through the gap between the window's bamboo shades.

Shahid stumbled into the doorway, tripping on his new sandals. "Mama?" he called, his smile as wide as his chubby cheeks would allow, his three-year-old eyes huge and sparkling. "Don't you sit on it!" he instructed as he fell into my arms, his belly laugh doing what it could to set things right, his brother right behind him. I looked up and the blazing sunlight pouring in between the window shades had bleached into almost nothing a painting that will soon hang in our home.

I don't find the photograph that reminds me of this moment until later, much later when our children are grown. But when I do, that Islamabad morning will come to mind immediately and effortlessly, as if places complement each other, like people sometimes do. The photograph is in my mother's childhood photo album, which is full of undersized images, all affixed with adhesive corners pulling away from the pages. At first, I'm transfixed by the sheet of light illuminating a portion rather than the man pouring wine or a woman's exultant laugh. I read my mother's caption, *Pa Eyck and Oma 1945,* and wonder at the selection of words, as if she had more than one father and the single year in which a world war ended said all there was to know about a celebration such as this. The photograph is of an evening in Minervaplein, my mother's childhood home in Amsterdam. Leo stands in the corner of his drawing room pouring wine and above him a Chinese porcelain plate hangs on the wall and dwarfs his head. Like the plate, Leo is bathed in light, but there is his smile not like my mother's and his curled fingers tight around the bottle he tips toward a crystal goblet. He cocks his head and looks at the camera from behind a row of seated guests. Oma, my mother's grandmother, peers into the camera; her look is stern, doubtful that the moment can be captured, oblivious that it will be frozen for posterity and a great-grandchild like me. In her caption, my mother didn't include her mother, Eleonora, whose back is toward us, her hair crimped for the occasion and the keyhole closure of her sheer dress dropping low in the hollow between her slender shoulder blades ablaze in the edge of light.

From the cocktail table, with the boys gathered in my arms, the Islamabad light dissolved the golden scene on a set of antique side tables my mother had inherited from hers and on which, I suspect, the liquor that 1945 evening was displayed. Like the cir-

cles of Oma's spectacles and the contours of the candle holders, my mother's words were precise. The *you children* and *your
father's children* were coupled, like Leo and his shadow, there in
the corner by themselves.

•

One day, my mother packed my father's two Samsonite suitcases and bought an airplane ticket. Then we sat in the kitchen
together while she broke the news that she was leaving. We all
pretended she would return, but the evidence of the house told
otherwise.

Mohammed had made a bonfire in the back lawn to which
he fed what my mother gave him: sheaves of our letters home,
utility bills, bank statements, documents that looked too official to burn, and the effluvia of twenty-seven years of accumulated paper. Fall had arrived, Naeem had returned to teaching in
Ithaca, our children had just started school a few streets away,
and the house was emptying. My father's closet was barren, but
so was hers. The drawers of the dresser my mother had inherited from my grandmother had once been filled with scarves and
medicines, perfumes and clip-on earrings, but they were now
empty. The bed was made with fresh sheets, as if not just my
mother, but my father, too, might rise from the dead to sleep
next to her again. A crocheted bedspread replaced the one she'd
set aside to take with her. Piles of belongings sprung up through
the house, each assigned to one of us. The living room furniture was pushed against the walls and in its place were the items
Ayesha would take with her on her move to Karachi. The things
that accumulated in what had recently become our parents'
library belonged to Omar. I'd packed dozens of boxes of books
for him after setting aside those I wanted (Agha Shahid Ali's
Half-Inch Himalayas, a rare copy in Islamabad when my mother
gave me the photocopy I still have) and those I might need for

future novels (*Birds of the Indian Subcontinent* and *Wildflowers of the Islamabad and Rawalpindi Districts*). Beside the cartons for which Omar would need to rent a California storage locker were a rolled up Chinese carpet, the dining room furniture, and our parents' slides (but not Bangladeshi ones). Another disassembled room was stacked with things my mother had given us, my childhood desk, her mother's crystal, the teak buffet, Oma's linen tablecloths, to which I added the red brown melted rock of a granite mountain. As shocking as the dissolution of our home seemed at the time, it was in the early stages yet. There was so much about loss and grieving that I didn't know.

My children made most things possible in those days (getting out of bed, for example) and my research was no exception. At their school, I met a journalist who connected me to West Pakistani soldiers who'd fought in East Pakistan during the 1971 war in which Bangladesh was born. I met them in Rawalpindi, a garrison town known as Islamabad's twin city, even though there's nothing analogous about them. Almost ten miles separate them, but like the Margallas in the opposite direction, Rawalpindi is a signpost for Islamabad's reach. Islamabad had not yet grown the pincers that surround Rawalpindi on the day when I sat with more than a dozen soldiers in the cramped and smoky office of an old and yellowed bungalow motel that was a remnant of the colonial era. I was surprised by men who appeared like any other (tall and short, round and lean, bearded and shaven, fit and not), which made it difficult to attach them to war or, in fact, anywhere else. While they may not all have been close friends, they were bound by the intimacy of war, and after several hours of repartee, they pulled me in. We laughed while we drank tea in marathon sessions that circled around but avoided details of horrible encounters: dentures falling out, untied pants falling down, facial expressions of soldiers caught in friendly fire. But most of it was misery, and eventually the circling stopped. Bloated bodies filled the waterways, bobbing in the rivers as if they still had some place to go. People were tied to trees for executions. Bridges were blown up, civilians were mown down. Genitalia were chopped off. Bengali women were brought to the barracks for soldiers to have their way with them. Taken aback by the casual suggestion of rape, I asked "Why?" and the soldier who'd spoken cleared his throat, lowered his head, and said he'd waited his whole life for someone to ask that question.

Ayesha called the motel manager in a panic during the first night of interviews because I was out so late. We'd just been served dinner on platters heaped with steaming rice and in bowls brimming with curry, and I reassured her in German, our secret language, as if there was something to hide. By the time I arrived at her home, all our children were asleep, and for the moment even my sister's newborn was quiet. I put my bag on a chair and reached for the ever-present pitcher of boiled water. I was exhausted. I hadn't slept much since my father died and was accustomed to the spinning ways of my mind when my body craved sleep that my mind refused to grant. This was not the same. I was bone-tired and deeply sad, but also oddly exhilarated.

As it happened, I needed those interviews with a desperation that shamed me. As soon as one interview ended, I looked forward to the next. The brutality filled me up. I felt myself expand with each story, become someone I'd never been. From being a stranger to horror, I became someone who lay down beside it every night. One cold October night, a tremor shook Islamabad. I was asleep in Noor's room when my dream absorbed the tremor as a bombing run on Dhaka airport, in which an interviewee (and I) watched his partner blown to pieces. The stories terrorized me, but they kept me awake to the world, alive to its possibilities, one of which was the future. When the soldiers spoke, I forgot my father's death, our dissolving house, the fact that Islamabad would never be my home again, the worry that I could not be Pakistani with him gone. Their stories kept me alive. I hid my interview notes on an empty shelf in an abandoned room, far from my children's reach so they would never know.

At the end of our stay in Islamabad, the closets, and everything else in the house, had been emptied. On the night of our departure, the suitcases were lined up in the carport waiting. Alone, I ran from room to room in a private goodbye ritual, dropping to my knee on the upstairs landing where an eleven-month-old Kamal had stumbled from my arms into my father's while learning to walk. We left the house, but not the city, for the final time.

Years later when we spoke of that wretched summer (but not then—or ever—of what she'd said), my mother suddenly remembered my interviews.

"What did the soldiers tell you?" she asked.

At *soldiers*, I forgot the ones I'd interviewed. I thought only of hers, the German soldiers who'd terrorized her when she waited in ration lines for bread or stood on the doorstep during searches for a forbidden radio that was concealed in a hollowed-out book and never found. I quickly realized my mistake, but it took me another few moments to find an answer.

"Well, what did they say?"

"Everything? Nothing?" I replied.

"Like anyone," she said and shrugged, and I wondered if she'd always been this wise.

SIX

After my father died, my mother chose Vienna again. She was sixty-five and had lived in Islamabad for twenty-seven years, longer than she'd lived (or would live) anywhere. A short stay in Amsterdam convinced her it had changed too much to ever again be home. She ruled out beginning again with any of her children, me in New York, Omar in California, or Ayesha in Pakistan. Vienna contained the promise of home because it had already been one; perhaps, because it was in a country that was neither hers nor his, it was where my parents had been happiest together. Upon her return, my mother embraced the city like a new lover, discovering it afresh every day. She walked cobbled streets near her Hohe Warte apartment to Grinzing, where she'd one day be buried, and beyond where, she'd say, the vineyards and Vienna Woods had been a salve for her loss. On other days, she walked the few miles downtown, where museums and concerts, and late in life, philosophy classes, sated her curiosity.

I, on the other hand, excised the city from my life as if I had no history with it—as if I hadn't been born there nor been a childhood resident nor visited as an adult. I threw it out of my life like the children's outgrown clothes. I made exceptions: Kamal was exempt from my travel ban one summer when he was ten and he visited my mother, and I exempted myself on the occasion of her seventy-fifth birthday when we all gathered in her home but I counted down the days (five) until I could leave again. I did not announce my intention never to return, at least not to anyone besides Naeem, but my mother knew.

Each time she invited me to visit, I'd respond, "But Mummy, why don't you come here?" and she did.

Years into turning down her invitations, she finally responded, "You're unreasonable."

I said nothing, so she added, "At least your attitude is unreasonable."

"Why?" I asked.

"The city isn't responsible for your father's death," she said.

"What is, then?" I asked, and she shook her head and let me be, until we had a similar conversation the following year and the one after that.

●

One January, after two decades of pretending otherwise, Naeem and I were reminded that we were not new to illness. Until then, the past had rubbed up against the present once a year in Naeem's routine medical tests, only to recede when his cardiologist delivered good results. Living, Naeem intuited, required distance from rather than surrender to illness, which is why he'd spent the months before it caught up with him on his bicycle, as if the miles he clocked and the hills he climbed assured more life. There were no assurances, however, and there was nothing he could do to keep the heart attack he'd had at thirty-three from catching up to him.

He was running on an unusually warm January day until he couldn't anymore. A crushing pain, like nothing he'd ever felt, crumpled him. His right ankle looked as it had when he'd started, not broken nor swollen, yet it was the locus of his pain. He spent a few days in the hospital, while blood thinners dissolved the blood clots in his leg and, most importantly, the large one in his heart, where blood had thickened against the rough of scar tissue. Early on, before he knew whether he could keep his leg (or his life) he'd asked to see the boys. Shahid sat in the chair farthest from Naeem, disinterested in details and saying little, wishing only for everything to have been as it was. The four years between the boys were never more evident and Kamal, in college by then, sat on his father's hospital bed and kissed him, wishing, too, that everything was as it had been, but knowing it could not be.

"Are you alone?" I'd asked when I called with news of his father's hospitalization.

"Does it matter? Tell me what you called to say," Kamal asked of me, steering me to the truth, that his father was terribly ill.

A few months later, in March, I called him again and didn't ask if he was alone. "Dad's in the hospital," I said, after I'd told his brother, who sat beside me. Naeem, while attending a conference in San Diego, had been taken by ambulance to a hospital where his racing heart had been shocked back to rhythm and a doctor who'd studied at Cornell was treating him. "I leave for San Diego in a few hours," I told him.

"Call me when you get there," he replied, parroting words I'd often said to him. The next morning, I spoke to Kamal before I spoke to my mother.

Like a cat with many lives, Naeem survived San Diego the way he'd survived Ithaca a few months earlier, and twenty years before that, Syracuse. Rochester, less than a two-hour drive away and home to the specialist who now treated Naeem for his newly arrived arrhythmias, became the center of his medical care until the right medication and the implantation of an ICD device would settle his heart. On each journey, I was reminded of the first time Naeem almost died. I'd flown over the thruway to Ravi Shankar and Rochester, Naeem's scribbled directions sliding over the dashboard. How young we'd been before death entered the register of our lives!

•

As she did every summer since my father died, my mother visited that summer of 2012 when Naeem was in and out of the hospital. My mother immediately noticed the hydrangeas that I'd planted in our backyard. I'd done so a few weeks earlier, when I was desperate for reminders of life, and they were already blooming.

"Hortensias," my mother said. "My mother's favorite flowers."

One morning, Naeem left for the office and my mother told me that she admired his resilience. She said she'd never heard him complain, not once in all these years, and she looked to him as an example. I listened to my mother long enough to consider that she, at seventy-nine years old, learned from my husband, and felt the world slightly off-kilter. But since Naeem's current illness, the long-ago Ravi Shankar concert was once again on my mind, so I shared my plan to research the Rochester concert.

"You want to do what?" she said.

"Is it odd I don't remember the concert?"

"But why would you, sweetheart? It was so long ago."

"His heart was dying, Mummy . . . music was playing."

She studied me with curiosity, as if I were crazy, which perhaps I was.

"He's alive. Think of that, my darling," she said, and caressed my cheek with the back of her hand before leaving the room.

A moment later, she returned with a yellow binder of genealogy materials intended for me. She'd inherited the materials from her sister who, a note in my aunt's handwriting indicated, gathered them in Room 15G in the New York Public Library. My mother flipped through the pages, marking names of immediate family members on the photocopied documents. The print was cramped and the pages were difficult to follow, so we did not study the binder for long.

There was a reason my mother had carried the binder into my home. We'd recently learned of a change in Dutch law that opened a route to Dutch citizenship, should I decide to pursue it. Until then, the same Napoleonic laws that had required my mother to obtain my grandfather's permission to marry had restricted my mother's ability to pass her citizenship to her eldest children; Ayesha was Dutch because of a decades-old amendment that had once applied to minors, but had been too late for me. In order to pursue the new option, I would need to trace the more recent genealogy of her family and collect as many of my mother's Dutch legal documents as possible.

My mother had already sent me one such document, which I pulled up on my laptop as we sat at the kitchen counter. She sighed when she saw it on the screen, and then she translated it for me: *Extract from the Register of Marriage Consents.*

"You children are damn lucky I saved any Dutch documents at all," she said.

"What do you mean?"

"After your father died, I gave the folder to Mohammed to put in the bonfire, but I changed my mind at the last moment."

While I stared at my grandfather's signature (an indecipherable, underlined slant), my mother was circumspect while she explained, again, the reason for such a document.

"He didn't want to sign it," she said, summing up in one sentence her struggle. "But the important thing for you children is that he did."

"For us?"

"You wouldn't be here otherwise."

"He didn't want you to marry? Or he didn't want you to marry Daddy?"

"Both I suppose," she said. "He didn't like that I was marrying someone from the East." She wouldn't reveal until a few weeks before her death that he'd referred to my father as *the Negro.*

My mother closed my laptop. "Let's forget about all that," she said and made coffee. Soon she was telling stories about her youth in Amsterdam.

She'd given incorrect directions to the German soldiers who'd stopped to ask her during the war. She and a friend skipped school more than once to watch ships come and go at Amsterdam's port. And when she was almost my age, she and her best friend made a prank call to her father's mistress. At the last story, which I'd never heard before, she laughed with infectious abandon.

"I would love to show the boys Amsterdam," she finally said.

"Well, why don't you?" I said.

"When? Next summer?

"What's wrong with now?" Kamal was already studying in Europe and Shahid was on summer break.

A few phone calls later, our frequent flier miles were spent, and we were researching hotels on Beethovenstraat, in my mother's childhood neighborhood.

A few weeks later, she sent me a postcard of Rembrandt's *The Jewish Bride* from the museum she'd visited with the boys.

"Isn't it beautiful?" she asked when we next spoke. "Those hands!"

"How big is it?" I wondered, unable to translate the palm-sized image into the painting.

"Big enough to love!" she said.

She mentioned Rembrandt's contemporaries, Aelbert Cuyp, Jan Steen, and Jan van Goyen, none of whose work I knew. My mother listed other paintings that she loved, few of which I recognized, but when she mentioned Vermeer, I remarked, "The Golden Age—" and she interrupted me.

"Listen to me. There was nothing *Goool-den* about it if you were a subject in a Dutch colony," she said, veering away from paintings and light. And soon we'd left behind *The Jewish Bride* for colonialism, the French atrocities in Algeria, the Dutch in Indonesia, and the British in India.

Rather than pay attention, I recalled that my mother had forbidden servants in our home when we were children in Islamabad. She'd been first to rise in the mornings to assure that a hot breakfast awaited us. When my father joined us at the kitchen table where she sat ready to pour tea, and he leaned over to kiss her good morning, I watched her be enveloped by color as much as by him.

"Do you know—" I interrupted my mother who was still outlining the atrocities of colonialism for me.

"Yes?"

"I once heard the boys say that you're the brownest person they know."

"I am! I am!" she said, so pleased.

•

It was late afternoon in New York and night in Vienna when she called a few months later. The onions in my wok were translucent, crushed garlic sizzled. We spoke often then, but not that often, or at least it seems so now. I turned off the stove and took the telephone into the bedroom, where I sat on the foot of the bed, above the small gap between the mattress and frame. The sky was leaden, the shade of November after autumn has dispensed with leaves and all that is left outside our bedroom window is the end-less shade that will carry us through winter and, hopefully, into another spring. She'd received the results of her bone marrow test and had them in her hand.

"Before we speak," my mother said, "you must promise not to look at your computer. Doctor's orders."

I left the bedroom to get my laptop and sat down again in time to hear her say she was fine, she would be fine, for a long time even, despite an imbalance in her bone marrow.

"Imbalance?" I asked.

Her bone marrow was misbehaving. She didn't have enough white blood cells because of a profusion of abnormal cells. "I have a condition," she said, "that's all."

She wouldn't admit "illness" until the end when nothing, not even *leukemia,* sufficed to describe what her body suffered. "I didn't know I'd become this sick," she'd whisper a week or two before her death, three years into the future.

"I've checked with the doctor and my condition is not genetic. You children have nothing to worry about."

I remember a sharpness falling through the window and bouncing off the mirror on the dresser, swallowed by the jewelry box she'd given me. Outside, cold air was readying itself for snow, the promise of what lay ahead. I'd been on this bed, looking at this light, thinking, *How much longer?* six months earlier, when Naeem's doctor said, "We cannot guess the future. We focus on today, which you are living." My mother was seventy-nine and I could guess the future.

"The treatment is chemotherapy," she said.

"You have cancer?" I asked.

"I'm not sick," she said.

A moment passed, and then another.

"Darling? You're on the computer, aren't you?"

A few weeks later, I visited my mother. A few months after that, I visited her again. And so it went.

•

She'd always loved the city above all, but my mother learned the history of Vienna better than almost anyone she knew. She pointed out buildings and rattled off facts each time we were in the tram and passed anything she thought worthwhile, which was often. It took several visits before I could will myself to feel interest.

My mother recounted the history of the Grand Hotel and pointed to the balcony of a room which used to be my father's office. She recalled the history of the Palais Ephrussi as we walked into the light-filled lobby and imagined what, if anything, had changed since it was depicted in our favorite memoir about Vienna, *The Hare with Amber Eyes*. We went to the Documentation Centre of Austrian Resistance housed in the old city hall and considered the glass display cases of clothing scraps and rotted Jewish identification cards placed opposite a large map of Vienna that depicted locations across the city (including near my mother's apartment) in which people with intellectual disabilities were confined during World War II. Downtown, near Hofburg palace, we looked at the pastries in the windows of Demel's Café and reminisced about chocolate cigars filled with whipped cream that had been an extravagant childhood treat.

"Let's ask if they have them," my mother said, giddy like a child, but I hesitated to allow the specialty, like the city, into my heart.

Instead, we walked a few blocks to Augustinerkirche, where the hearts of Habsburg royalty are stored in urns, and afterwards, to the Kaisergruft, where their bodies are stored, except for the intestines which, for reasons my mother didn't explain, are in the catacombs below Stephansdom, Vienna's signature cathedral, also a quick walk away. I remember being sympathetic to the Habsburg ritual of sprinkling the dead here and there across the city, filling place with monuments to the dead. My father, too, was dismembered, in bits and pieces of memory, across time zones, safe wherever his wife and children reside.

That evening, my mother waved in the direction of a living room cabinet in her Vienna apartment.

"I should burn them," she said.

"Burn what?"

"The letters. You children have no business reading your parents' correspondence."

It was the first I'd heard of letters between my parents and I wanted to know more, but that was all she'd say.

"Honestly, I really must," she said, and I half expected her to get up right then and do it.

She was right, of course, but I begged her not to, and then didn't think of them again.

Every year, my mother visited my father's last place on earth on the same two days. The last place she ever saw him or held his hand was the Viennese Hospital called Krankenhaus Hietzing, so she went there on his death anniversary and on All Souls' Day, an Austrian Catholic holiday which honors the dead. In the fifteenth year after his death, my mother visited the hospital a third time, and that was to accompany me in my need to visit the memory.

It was a brilliant July day, the kind in which blue pours from the sky, but my mother was eighteen months into a six-month prognosis of her illness and she was covered in purple bruises. In the hollow of her bones, inside the sponge of her bone marrow, red and white blood cells were being outnumbered by abnormal cells. She was a week out of her second course of chemotherapy, a tortuous regimen that kept her in the hospital one week of every month weighed down by intravenous lines and injections that left her limbs permanently battered. At the time of our visit, seven days after discharge, her still swollen wrist was wrapped in gauze where a vein had been prodded with one too many needles and collapsed.

Once, my mother had been five foot ten without heels, slightly taller than my father, comfortably taller than her daughters, and even her son, until he returned from two years of college. In the years after my father's death, she'd shed inches, until her youngest grandchildren caught up to her. All the while, she retained her long, confident stride, and she filled her seat at a table the way she filled a room. While illness took its time with her, wartime Amsterdam tailed her, tightening its steel grip. As it was for my whole life, she jumped at loud noises and smaller ones too, but when her illness progressed, so did her panic: at house keys misplaced, at emails unanswered, and always, at the prospect of food spoiling.

On the day of our visit, on a sidewalk which followed grooved tram rails, my mother's usual swift pace slowed to a crawl. Minutes before the hospital appeared, my mother suddenly clutched my arm, her hands strong as ever. Her neatly penciled eyebrows rose and the rims of her eyelids flooded with pink. "Where. Is. It?" she asked, struggling to catch her breath, afraid she'd lost her way. The journey, like her illness, had exhausted her, and I wondered if she was becoming a truer version of herself.

Except for being renamed to reflect the district in which it resides, Krankenhaus Hietzing was as I remembered from when my father lay dying: grand like most of Vienna's architecture. It lies close to the Vienna Woods, on the southern banks of the Vienna River and near Schönbrunn, a former Habsburg palace to which the world's oldest zoo is connected and where Kamal once devoured an ice cream cone while watching two rhinoceros play. A fleet of Mercedes Benz taxis waited at the gates as if it were a five-star hotel, and for a moment I forgot people were dying inside. We passed the first building in the hospital's pavilion design, where a friend had delivered my parents the day my father was admitted. Slightly beyond in the second pavilion, Charles had read my father's final lung scans in the radiology department. The courtyard was awash in mounds of gold and violet flower beds, but my mother was distracted by the top floor of a distant building. I looked up and a memory rushed into my body, feet first. I'd forgotten. I, too, had been a patient in this hospital.

Three years before my father's death, I'd spent two weeks at the hospital recovering from a lung infection. Finally pregnant after trying for a year, I was terrified of miscarrying. Naeem, Kamal, and I were passing through Vienna on the way back to New York from Islamabad, at the behest of my parents who were visiting. I'd been sick for days, downing baby Aspirins in the hope that they were safe for my pregnancy and would quiet the growing rattle in my lungs. I'd chewed through Kamal's emergency supply, and when I began to wake up drenched in sweat and unable to eat, I knew I would not make my flight two days away. I was admitted to then Lainz hospital where my father's friend, a doctor, worked. When he came to see me, I was too weak to put on my glasses. He and his attending students were a blur, but I remembered being supported in a sitting position while he thumped my back to elicit sounds from my lungs. "What have you done to yourself?" he asked softly, and even if I'd had a voice, I had no reply. When a team of doctors eventually identified the intravenous antibiotics that would make me well, the medicine burned like fire through my veins.

My mother waved at the window through which I'd watched Naeem and Kamal enter and leave the courtyard. "Remember?" my mother asked, pleased to offer what I'd forgotten. I smiled for her, but the memory of my hospital stay was one of the saddest of my life. I'd had to use a bedpan because I didn't have the strength to walk to the bathroom or steady myself on the toilet. Early every morning, Naeem came to the hospital to bathe me, holding me in the shower and lathering me with soap, my body thinner than it had ever been as an adult, despite the possibility of life clinging inside. Kamal was initially forbidden to visit, and then required to wear a mask for protection. Naeem lifted him on the bed and put him in my arms, but I could not wrap them around him and the pressure of his face in my shoulder was unbearable. It had been the summer I'd fought with my parents as if I was a teenager again. They could not tolerate the idiosyncrasies of a three-year-old boy—loud and rambunctious, exuberant with life in every way—or my parenting—too lenient, they said. We'd fought from morning to night in Islamabad, a routine that continued unabated in Vienna. I counted the days and then hours until we'd be in our own home again and when my illness interfered, I lay in my hospital bed and sucked on tricolor popsicles, all I could eat, and begged the doctor to discharge me until, after two solid weeks, he finally did.

"Yes, I remember," I told my mother as we walked side by side.

At the steps to the cardiology building, I detailed my research for my mother. The one-hundred-year-old hospital spread over several acres was built by Vienna's Christian socialist mayor, Karl Lueger, now a controversial figure because of Nazi sympathies. Before it was named Hietzing (when my father died) or Lainz hospital (when I was hospitalized), it was named Emperor's Jubilee hospital, in commemoration of Emperor Franz Joseph I. The hospital is famous for the Angels of Death, four nurse's aides who killed up to 200 elderly patients in the 1980s. They did so by administering lethal doses of insulin and tranquilizers, and by pouring water down patients' windpipes and drowning them. Like my mother, I'd been relieved to learn they were in jail during my father's stay. His death had been the fourth in the hospital's almost one thousand bypass surgeries that year, but the total number of deaths we don't know. In trying to make sense of the sepsis that killed him three weeks after surgery, I'd stumbled upon the obtuse fact that a necktie can transmit bacteria, and in Austria where doctors in teaching hospitals are formally addressed as Herr Doktor Professor, the world-renowned surgeon who operated on my father and lives in my mind always wears a tie.

"Quite possible," my mother said, because the surgeon haunted her as well.

Inside the building, as in life, I depended on my mother for my bearings. I'd been the last in our family to arrive in Vienna, met at Schwechat airport by Omar who told me that my father was still alive, but not for long. The cardiology floor was more compact, less imposing than in my memory. I took photographs while my mother explained that my father had been on the third floor before emergency surgeries shifted him. At a patient-only elevator with ancient collapsing gates, I imagined what my father, momentarily or forever asleep, had looked like inside it. A friendly nurse dressed in a Brazilian soccer jersey for the evening's World Cup match appeared in a hallway. Behind her was the heavy steel door of a recurring dream. We followed her into a supplemental waiting room, but the closeness of the door, the fact that it was within reach, extinguished my need to confirm the glass cubicle just inside. There, my father had lain on a special mattress while a ventilator breathed Darth Vader breaths and tubes grew like supple twigs from his swollen body.

We fell into matching chairs, unaware if people wandering about were visitors or staff. I glanced at the wall directory of medical professionals on duty in the cardiac ICU, and my mother observed the absence of the famous heart surgeon who'd retired long ago. As was her habit, my mother pretended she'd never liked him, despite the fact that she and my father had been overly enthusiastic for him before everything went wrong. I watched her hands, remembering they'd sewed my prom dresses, as she spoke and they gestured. She said she would never forgive the scoundrel, not for my father's death (in God's purview, she said), but because the surgeon had not condoled with her.

"Do doctors do that sort of thing?" I wondered aloud, and for all her fragility, anger flashed across her face.

Before we left the grounds, we found the hospital's fourth pavilion, the Chapel of Holy Trinity. The chapel was surprisingly bright and airy with walls of stained-glass windows, one of which featured St. John Nepomuk, the same saint of bridges after which the small church on the corner of Hofzeile, my childhood street, was named. The floor was tiled in white squares and black diamonds, and Jesus healed the sick in a triptych behind the altar. The Bible lay open to the story of Abraham, a detail I documented with another photograph. We dropped coins into a collection tin and lit candles for our dead: my father, my mother's mother, her sister, my father's sister, his mother, his father, his brothers. Our list was longer than ever, and until he'd joined it, my father had participated in the ritual without remarking on the oddity of Muslims honoring their dead in a church. My mother struggled with the last candle and when the wick stopped flickering, she said, "That's enough," and stood. We left and as I held open the door, I wondered if Confraternität, the hospital in which she was being treated and where, presumably, she would die, had a chapel.

I'd survived my father's dying, which made it possible that I would survive hers. On the journey home, with her beside me breathing through a crumpled tissue to keep germs at bay, I thought back to what had been. In the months after his death, he'd disrupted my sleep more than my babies ever did. For two years, I awoke at 3:55 in the morning and waited for 4:00, the time of his death, to arrive. I rarely fell asleep again, but if I did, it was the sleep of the dead, and when my day began, I was only partially in it, unable to dislodge from slumber. The night after our hospital visit, I slept more deeply and for longer than I could have hoped, but when I awoke and remembered my father, and then my mother, it was 4:00 all over again and I hadn't slept at all.

SEVEN

On a February afternoon in 2016, when darkness falls in Vienna before the day is done, my mother and I rode the tram to a favorite restaurant on the edge of downtown. The short walk from the station was ragged until I slipped my arm into hers and surrendered to an unfamiliar, labored pace. At the restaurant, her gaunt face was made radiant by candlelight that filled in her thinned eyebrows. The silver table settings, too elaborate for our meal, added to a celebration of sorts, which meals with her were in her final months. Our conversation veered from topic to topic before arriving at my writing. She was pleased I'd written a new essay, but at mention of the title, "5 Queen's Road," she cried out as if she'd been struck.

"Not again!" she said, invoking my novel of the same name. "You must find something else to write about! Something that doesn't have to do with family."

"Like what?" I teased.

She slapped the table and her wedding ring rang out. She hadn't removed it when my father died and wouldn't until a few weeks before her death when she wiggled it off her swollen finger for Ayesha to keep.

The waiter set down our sparkling apple juice and the votive candle on the starched tablecloth flickered. My mother ignored me when I explained that the essay didn't feature her. "You know I don't like the way I am in your novel," she said, as if she divided her time between Vienna and my most recent book, *City of Spies*. Her complaint was old, as was her conflation of my fiction with our lives, but in those last months, besides longing for her to live, I wanted to be a kinder, more understanding daughter, so I was still and listened. "I don't curse like that," she was saying about an earlier novel. "You should know better. And what do you think? When I was pregnant with your brother, I lay around all day in the garden of 5 Queen's Road, as if your father didn't need help doing anything?" In the candlelight, she was not yet eighty-two, but thinner than ever, amplified by perfect posture which age and illness could not defeat. That day's haircut softened her face, and no one but us would have known that chemo had ruined her fine hair. She tapped her index finger against the glass and, as I often did, I caught myself trying to memorize her, as if a lifetime of being her daughter hadn't already committed the breadth of her fingers, so much like mine, to my mind. Our Wiener schnitzels arrived and she pierced a lemon wedge with her fork, and I don't remember why, but the conversation shifted.

Back in her apartment, Lahore greeted us in copper trays leaning side by side in the entryway and a silk carpet set at an angle on the parquet—all before we reached the living room. We did not need the reminders, for the place was on our minds.

"I'd never seen anything like it," my mother said, when I kissed her goodnight.

I sat on her bed and fiddled with her radio until it was set on a volume that suited her and would not wake me in the other bedroom. I pulled her bedsheet to her chin, as she'd grown to like, and waited.

"5 Queen's Road was a circus," she said, her eyes closed, trying to put a chapter to rest. "Don't tell Munir," she whispered, as if I could.

I left Vienna for Islamabad the next day, and she wished she could come with me. Vienna was what Islamabad was not, yet like a woman still torn in two directions seventeen years after she'd left, she continued to long for her dogs, the house, those hills. "Back home . . . ," she'd say, which had kept us on our toes at first, but slowly we realized that in the speaking of it, Islamabad was still home, but in the living of it, Vienna was.

"Give the hills my love," she said wistfully when we hugged goodbye, and when I saw her again in a few weeks, she asked, "So, how were they?" as if she was also missed.

•

The landscape of my mother's world shifted; where it had once leaped unbound from continent to continent, it became finite, reduced to her apartment and what she could observe from its windows. Kahlenberg, Bald Mountain, was as far as she could see. The gentle mountaintop a few miles beyond was a fixture of her Vienna, and when my mother returned alone to the city, she'd climbed it more than once to gaze at the sweep of the city and the Danube. For all the detail she imparted about Vienna (the oldest zoo, an emperor's café, Roman ruins) she did not reveal Kahlenberg's surprise: three hundred years earlier, when Aelbert Cuyp, still alive, had stopped painting, it was the site where a Polish king beat back Turkish forces.

Until she couldn't, she filled her head with other worlds. Orhan Pamuk's *A Strangeness in My Mind,* about Istanbul, a city that she loved, sat on the windowsill near her bed, a bookmark two thirds of the way through the small print, her name, *Thera Khan,* inside the cover. The book was too heavy for her to hold and too dense for a weakening mind to grasp, and in concession to her illness, she didn't take it to the hospital for the last time or return to it upon release. Instead, she began Colm Tóibín's slim *The Testament of Mary,* which fit more easily in her hands, but not in her mind. Her eyelids fell as she read, relinquishing her grip on the story and our world at the same time. "It's about Jesus' mother," Ayesha reminded her, but neither the novella nor reference to the religion she'd renounced kept her in the story or our lives.

The past, always part of her landscape, was steadfast as ever. Her mother's black and white portrait hung in the study. My grandmother Eleonora died in June of 1959, at forty-nine, before we could know her, but she'd filled our home in Vienna or Islamabad as if we did. Eleonora was forever black and white, fixed in youth and beauty as she was in family lore, where she resided without nuance: wronged, loved, missed. Until cancer robbed my mother of tears, a casual mention of her could fill my mother's eyes, as if her mother had died the week before in Vienna, not decades earlier in Amsterdam. Sometimes when we were children in Islamabad, in the wake of another June death anniversary, we'd catch my mother alone and staring blankly, with her feet tucked under her on a sofa beneath a ceiling fan, and we'd know our grandmother was in the room. When she spent summers with us in New York, and she awoke remote and unapproachable in my home, I'd register the date and hush my children as we'd hushed ourselves.

As my mother rested on the living room sofa and her rice paper skin shed flakes on blue leather grain, Kahlenberg lay behind her. The radiator clunked mysterious sounds and a basket of pinecones she'd collected stopped scenting the air. Out of sight, an Indonesian table runner quivered in the breeze of the kitchen door when I checked on the spinach soup. All the while, the fabled painting she'd bought in Islamabad kept watch. As she grew smaller and more translucent beneath it, the painting, almost as wide as she was tall, grew more lush, as if the life leaving her rose into it, elevating the yellows, blues, and greens so they were bolder still. Lying there, she might have stretched her shrunken arm to graze the canvas and remembered the day she bought it.

•

Soon, the only thing thriving in her body was cancer. It stunned her with jolts of pain ("like electricity," she said) in her arms and in her belly, and robbed her of her pleasures. Daily walks were the first to go, then lunches with friends, followed by music and television in quick succession. She gave up food too, but we didn't allow her this. At our behest (and now regret), the doctor prescribed appetite stimulants. The pills made her eat little, greedily. Every evening for dinner, she consumed egg salad toast, but only if it was topped with sliced pickle, as if it made perfect sense for her pregnancy craving to return in death's proximity. Her interest in books did not wane. She clung to *The Testament of Mary* as she drifted away from us, as if giving up on the written word was tantamount to giving up on life.

I kept my now published essay to myself, along with the news that it had reached Lahore. At a literary festival a month earlier, a woman had waved the essay at me. Close behind was a man who introduced himself as the grandson of Dina Nath, the owner of 5 Queen's Road. My breath caught with surprise, but also delight, and I meant it when I said I was happy to meet him.

He hesitated before he shook my hand and pulled me toward him. "Your grandfather was not my grandfather's tenant!" he exclaimed once and then repeatedly.

"What was he then?" I finally asked.

He chronicled other inaccuracies in the essay: His parents were murdered in a land, not business, dispute, his father was not a jeweler—he did not work, Dina Nath died years before I said he did so I could not have planned to interview him, and I'd been wrong about when the house was built. All the while, several of my cousins, whose parents had also lived in 5 Queen's Road, waited for me in the audience out of earshot.

Home in Ithaca, I remembered what I'd forgotten, the family interviews I'd recorded two decades earlier while researching my novel. Listening on an old Walkman, I hear myself tell an aunt that I'd almost interviewed Dina Nath's Muslim son, not Dina Nath, and one of my mistakes, at least, is obvious. By then, I'd written the grandson an apology and asked if there were more inaccuracies, as if a finite list would settle the matter. His subsequent inventory included claims that my grandfather never paid rent, as a judge he'd influenced unrelated litigation that involved Dina Nath's family, and my grandfather had been supplied with furnished living quarters, a detail that worried me the most.

Later, I searched for answers in the recordings Omar made at the end of my mother's life when the three of us kept her company in her apartment and at her hospital bedside. I listened to my mother reminisce about the 5 Queen's Road she knew and confuse details in my novel with those in her memory.

"The girls buried jewelry in the flowerpots on the roof," she said, and I hear myself correct her, "Mummy, that's my novel and not life."

After a moment of confusion, she chuckled. But she speaks with calm clarity when she states, "That house was full of characters."

My mother's Oma says something similar, not of 5 Queen's Road, but it fits just as well. In a letter to my mother in Chicago, she writes about their relatives, *The dear Lord has strange tenants.*

Although I considered it, I did not share my experience of Dina Nath's grandson with my mother on the morning I walked into her hospital room and awakened her from a dream. I squeezed lemon into her water because without it, she couldn't drink, and without water, she couldn't speak. Her speech was slow, her words drawn out, as if her words, like her, were clinging to life. In her dream, she'd received a telephone call from Lahore and on the other end of the staticky line was a voice she did not recognize. The caller was offended by something her family member had written about his family. She'd shrugged off his complaint and put down the ancient black telephone receiver, but lying in her bed, she tossed against her pillows and struggled with the wand-like hospital bed controls. Her verb tenses skipped back and forth in the way past, present, and future mingle in closeness to death. She declared the dream a premonition, and recalled another one: the time she and my father boarded a PIA flight and she told a flight attendant that the elderly man in the front of the plane would die in flight, and he did.

"Why did I say that? I wouldn't dream of saying that in my common mind," she marveled before pointing at me and returning to 5 Queen's Road. "When he confronts you—" she said, presumably mustering her uncommon mind. She was calm again and just when I thought she'd lost her words, she found them. "Apologize and rectify," she added, taking breaths between syllables, transforming her instructions into an almost-rhyme.

Her eyelids dropped and I wanted to tell her that in the present, her premonition was already the past. But in that moment, sorting out time, laying it flat like a map so we might locate ourselves, was beside the point. Instead, I was consumed by a single thought: Was my grandmother's dresser—the one I'd played with as a child and filled with scarves and perfumes as an adult— Dina Nath's? My mother slept, and underneath the bedsheets, her chest rose and fell and rose and fell as if it always would, and I kept my question, with my secret, to myself.

•

Near the end, after she'd had her bout with edema and her swollen back returned to its natural size, and she was small enough for us both to lie on her narrow hospital bed, my mother would say this only once. "I'm so sorry, my darling, that when I die this city will have another stain on it for you."

My mother said other things frequently, so we wouldn't forget.

"Eat the food that's in the refrigerator. Before going out," she said, despairing of waste as she always did because she'd been trained by war.

"I'm not brave," my mother said. "I live like we all do. I hope for tomorrow."

"You children. No fighting. When I'm gone," she warned from her hospital bed, raising her finger and shaking it at us as she'd done when we were children.

"I'm not afraid," she said, and then again, "I am. *Not. Afraid.*"

Time elongated. Instead of being all around and everywhere, it assumed shape. It lengthened to accommodate as much or as little as was needed. Whether slow or fast, stopped or started, it moved toward her end, whittling her body, sharpening her bones, loosening her skin as if readying her for flight. Time was the slender neck of a vase on a spinning wheel.

In her own hospital room in the Josefstadt district of Vienna, my mother said she couldn't explain the sensation, only that it was strange to be so close to death. "It's right here. Soft, waiting," she said dreamily, lifting a bruised and swollen hand to suggest it was within reach. She described the walls of her hospital room falling in like curtains in a breeze. She claimed to have had visitors (or at least wisps of them) clad in white and swaying over her, but they disappeared if she reached for them. "I've just been in another world," she would say, and I wondered if she was testing her footing and returning to us so we recognized its nearness.

One afternoon I sat on her bed holding her hand and we chatted about everyday things, a shoe sale at the tram stop around the corner, whether the jet-black hair of her favorite nurse's aide was dyed, and how her doctor found time to train for a half marathon.

After a pause in which she slept for a few minutes, she tugged my hand and whispered, "Now you can write about another hospital."

The speed of my response surprised me, as did the childish expression I used, which I borrowed from my toddler children when they'd eaten enough. "All done," I said, unclasping my hand from hers. I had no desire to chronicle her coming death the way I had my father's a few years earlier, when together she and I returned to the hospital where he'd died. I didn't intend to write about Confraternität, though eventually that's exactly what I do. The hospital was founded in the 1800s, it has ninety-six beds, and it sits across the street from several tram tracks, a Café Aida, and a Triumph underwear shop. The modest hospital restaurant pairs breaded turkey cutlets with a spectacular poppy seed salad dressing, and it lies only one floor above a basement corridor that leads to a room with a stainless steel refrigerator that is long like a coffin and low to the ground awaiting the corpse.

Later that day, I took my mother from her third-floor hospital room to ground level so she could sit in the courtyard and feel the breeze on her skin. She'd refused a wheelchair and hobbled into the elevator with her walker. The exertion depleted her and as the doors closed, she slumped back, but because she'd lost the ability to judge distance, she imagined the side of the elevator as farther away than it was. My mother's head fell hard against it and just then, I imagined her dead, fallen out of our world.

When we returned to her hospital room, my mother required care more intimate than she could bear. Back in her bed, with the three of us looking at her, waiting, she said, "This is no way to live," and begged us to see Caravaggio's paintings in the Kunsthistorisches Museum. "Go!" she said, as if paintings might save us all.

It was June again when my mother died, four days before my grandmother's fifty-seventh death anniversary. Her hospital room was quiet, falling rain the only music to accompany her. I was boarding an airplane in Newark, too late, this time, for a final goodbye. Ayesha told me that in the disquiet that accompanied her end, my mother fretted over the date of her mother's death anniversary, as if she could not bear to leave it behind. Much left her mind, settling just outside it, barely out of grasp. Was the anniversary yet to come or had it already passed? I could not fathom her loss until I visit her in the morgue and see that she, too, left the country of the living for that of the dead, and there it was: naked, illimitable. Now, when I think of her on the sofa of my Islamabad childhood with the ceiling fan laboring above, I dream it otherwise, and I sink beside her and fold her into my arms in the precise way I long for her to hold me now.

There is no fighting.

Before we go to restaurants, we eat what is in the refrigerator.

We spend the next twelve days settling all that needs to be settled. It is so much. Between the three of us, we divide up my parents' paintings, the copper, Oma's remaining linens. In our steady dispersal of her things, we reach the cabinet she'd waved toward and my parents' letters are waiting.

Then, before we leave Vienna, the three of us stand in front of Caravaggio's *Rosenkranzmadonna*. I study the immense red drape —like sky—hanging over a scene of grace. I recall her description at death's doorstep, *Walls falling in like curtains in a breeze,* and I imagine her sailing far beyond the drape and all of us.

EIGHT

My parents' letters crossed the Atlantic one last time. At home in Ithaca, when I unpacked the binder from my bag, it slipped to the floor and fell open to one of my father's letters. For an instant, his handwriting catapulted me to my past, cards received, forms signed, lists made. I didn't want to, but I read a single line in the middle of the sky-blue page. *I feel so sorry I cannot be with you, my love,* my father wrote my mother in Amsterdam a few days after her mother's death. He was far away in Seoul for work and she was twenty-five with a baby on her hip, dismantling her family home. I closed the binder more harshly than I intended and did not open it again for a year.

Instead, I studied her photo albums, where the person at the end of her life does not resemble the one in the photographs. In my house, they sit as they did in hers: between her mother's childhood photographs and documents of her distant past, as if carefully organizing evidence of her life had helped her—as it would us—make sense of it. But I find traces of her illness, anyway, because she'd leafed through the pages shortly before dying. In the scratchy handwriting of her final weeks, she added wobbly captions where there had been none. She wrote the names of her grandparents and parents next to their photographs, a nod to how little we would know without her. At the back of one album, my father's handwriting is preserved in images of a family tree they'd made and he'd photographed, and I recognize in them his habit of photographing museum plaques for future reference. I imagine her near the end of her life, with the annotated photo album in her lap and the letters within reach, revisiting her desire to burn the letters. But by then, prying open the binder's rings and freeing letters from their slippery sleeves would have been exacting work—her once strong hands unsteady like the rest of her.

A few months later, Naeem and I hung the Gulgee painting that does not depict the shahada on the single wall in our home that could accommodate a canvas that large. I passed it several times a day, and I read the shahada often. One afternoon, intent on locating each word of it, I settled on the sofa and considered the painting alongside multiple calligraphic renderings I have found in books and online. At close study, the shahada was nowhere to be found. I took a photograph of the painting and sent it to a friend, an Islamic scholar, who consulted others before returning the verdict. Not only was it not the shahada, the individual letters (if that is what they were) did not amount to words.

"It's nonsense?" I conferred with Naeem.

"It's abstract," he said.

Frustrated, I thought, *Same thing*.

When I speak to the painter's son, Amin, also an artist, he tells me that when his father looked at his work, he saw a moment of his life. Ismail Gulgee, the Pakistani painter, was my father's age, and he too is dead. Amin explains that the painting is a precursor to his father's calligraphic work, when he was not yet using his paintbrush as a quill. His strong brushstrokes are gestural, all energy and motion, and as Amin talked, I imagined his father's gestures arrested in the tracks and grooves of raised paint.

Expansive brushstrokes mimic a shoulder's range of motion as they spill down the right side of the canvas and elongate across the bottom. What falls on the right is lifted on the left, where smaller, less defined strokes are muffled in a rush of pointillism. Restrained characters emerge at the top where they pretend at language and tempt with meaning. The vast middle is a sea of soft shadows and yellow green. It is loosely framed by scattered bursts of gold leaf, each spectral, and one larger than my hand.

When I look at the painting, I see my mother's life. It is dated 1972, the year we moved to Pakistan. I see Thera standing there at the Art Galleries, in her batik dress, willing herself into the painting and her new life.

•

My mother is always sick when she visits my dreams, which is how it is a year later, the night before I read the letters. She wears a flowing hospital gown that swallows her disappearing frame and she doesn't smile, not even when we're on Währinger Straße, seated in a café I don't recognize. We drink melanges and share hazelnut cake, both slathered with whipped cream. She hardly speaks, and when she does, it's a whisper.

"Try to be brave," she says.

I have a voice, but I whisper too. When I wake up, I don't remember what I said.

She waits with me in my study as I read the letters.

When I read them for the first time, I've already organized them further, placing the nineteen months of correspondence into chronological order and freezing my parents in conversation. The letters are written on blue aerogrammes and onion skin paper, and sometimes white linen letter pads, and on all surfaces, they stretch with longing and constrict with details. My mother's voice rises as I follow her words with my fingertips; it is as I remember it, loud and strong, as if it does not lie still with the rest of her in an Austrian cemetery, where her gravestone has a triangulated view of a church, vineyard, and cityscape.

Blinding snow lowers the afternoon sky until it touches my window. She, Thera, is alive again. I hear her ask my father, *You don't think I have a mind?* who replies by returning her angry letter with his own so she can see for herself how she has hurt him. Many letters chronicle their months of separation before they married, she in Amsterdam, he mostly in Chicago. They see each other only twice, in the same month, when my father visits on the way to and from Lahore. Bereft at his departure, my mother writes, *I was too choked to cry. It's like someone tears me apart when I say goodbye to you.*

I stow the letters in a drawer. Every so often, I shuffle through them: 17 December 1955 or 3 January 1957, each letter evidence of who they were long before me. The past is a place I've received from my parents and each time I read a letter, I visit them there. Amsterdam, Chicago, Lahore. The letters cement their relationship across continents, perhaps the least of their divides. In one letter, my mother is furious with my father for suggesting he seek permission from her father to marry. *After all I've told you, after all he has done and taken, you ask?*

The letters between them dwindle to a trickle in 1959 when her mother is dying. My parents are married by then and she chronicles her mother's decline in broad strokes in intermittent letters to my father who is away for work and upset not to receive one every day. *There's no more hope,* she finally informs him by telegram. My father, meanwhile, has just been to Pakistan and consulted a palmist. He has already posted his letter with the man's prediction, that her mother will be saved, her father will return to them, their family will be whole again. My mother does not respond to this, but I imagine she has the palmist in mind when she writes my father some weeks later, *Where is God?*

The letters are an outline rather than a chronicle of their time apart. Onion skin paper and aerogrammes are limited in what they can hold. I do not know if my father ever learned the details of my grandmother's last days, but I did. Omar finds interviews he recorded with our mother and aunt. The tapes are so old that when I finally listen to them, my college-bound niece gurgles as a newborn. What my mother claims in vague and insufficient terms, my aunt specifies with exact and abundant detail. My mother declares it an awful time between deep sighs, and then repeats herself, as if repetition renders the enormity of loss. In contrast, my aunt's account is vivid, technicolor, and she delivers my terminally ill grandmother in 1950s Amsterdam back to almost-life.

Virtually blind from lupus by then, Eleonora lay in her daughters' cramped childhood bedroom because she refused to return to the bed she'd shared with her husband. The room was packed with floor-to-ceiling cherry cupboards interrupted by a mirror and basin and two twin beds that folded up into the wall, only one of which was in use. The French doors opened to a five-inch step, a bit of gravel, and a north-facing triangular courtyard in which she'd planted pink and blue hydrangeas, her favorite flowers, and two Japanese cherry trees, which bloomed like clockwork in the shade come spring. The curtains were tightly drawn and the doors firmly closed, but my grandmother screamed in fright if she suspected a shadow of light filtering under the door, at which Lola, the poodle, barked like mad. For a while, my aunt slept surreptitiously on the floor next to her mother, but before her mother slipped into a coma, her senses heightened and she ordered her daughter out. In the end, during the sixteen days it finally took her to die, my aunt's friend, a nurse, moved in to help, rolling my grandmother one way and then the other to change the sheets on the narrow bed, bringing expertise to the exhausting labor of attending a life at its end. The children kept their promise to their mother and she died at home.

After I read the letters and listen to the recordings, I find *Fragments from the Diary of a Bachelor*. It's a poem, a wedding gift from Leo's brother to the bride and groom and a keepsake for their guests. Eleonora and Leo's marriage failed, but their courtship survives on the stained yellowed pages bound by a frayed thread that sit on my desk where the gift is now mine.

The poem confirms the only details of my grandparents' courtship that I've been told (their first meeting in Maastricht, my great-grandfather's misgivings about their relationship, a car accident that changed everything) and expounds on one. Leo first saw Eleonora in a jewelry store where he was attempting to sell items from his silver business. Eleonora left, but she forgot her umbrella, and the jeweler, uninterested in Leo's wares, twisted a Dutch idiom to refer to Eleonora as a gold rooster: rich, beautiful, and young. Leo asked for her address, and the jeweler, who was acquainted with Eleonora's family, promptly shared it. Later the same day, Leo stood at Eleonora's doorstep with her forgotten umbrella and his arms full with roses.

Fourteen years her senior, Leo swept Eleonora off her feet. She was seventeen, fresh from boarding school in England, and thrilled with the attention of a handsome and sophisticated suitor who drove a car. Leo was an immaculate dresser and a good dancer too, and he introduced her to a nightlife of restaurants and parties that she'd never known as the daughter of a *notaris*. She was shy and he was not, and at seventeen, she was confidently ushered into a new world. With the help of the brother who commissioned their wedding poem, Leo followed her on family holidays to resorts in Aachen, Germany, and Engelberg, Switzerland, where they secretly met, while Eleonora's father thought he was putting much needed distance between them so that his daughter would see she'd fallen for Leo too hard, too quickly. Nothing anyone said to her, neither her parents nor friends, changed her mind. Leo was in a car accident soon thereafter, and the doctors said he was going to die. On the way to the hospital, her father, a man of his word, softened in the face of her sobs and promised that if he lived, she could marry him. He did, so they married, Leo thirty-four and Eleonora twenty.

The poem, fragmented as it is, is augmented by my aunt's recollections, which I listen to again and again. Eleonora was an only child and her father was her center, even after she married

Leo and moved to Amsterdam. But her father never visited when Leo was home, possibly because he could never make peace with the marriage or, perhaps, because he knew that Leo had already taken a lover. Eleonora and Leo's relationship was unhappy almost from the start, even as they had three children, each two years apart. When my mother was born, they gave her older brother to his grandparents to raise in Maastricht. My mother and aunt either did not realize or did not remember this fact until they all had children of their own and their brother pointed it out: he'd always had his own room in Minervaplein, but he didn't return until he was thirteen or fourteen after their grandparents' Maastricht home was bombed and required it. My mother may not have remembered the absence of her brother, but one of her first memories is sitting on the toilet as a three-year-old, overhearing a conversation between her mother and her grandfather. "I should have listened to you," Eleonora wept, "and now I have three children." And when her father died after the war, she was never the same again—and neither was her marriage.

Toward the end of his life, Eleonora's father entrusted her with a letter to be opened after his death. She stored it in a secret compartment in a writing desk bulging with drawers and locks that once entertained her small children. The letter informed her of his wish to be cremated, which he knew his wife, a devout Catholic, would not like. He explained that his wife was his sole inheritor and he added a specific caveat, that she must arrange her finances so that his son-in-law would never gain access. After the cremation, the two women, one old and one young, quietly set out to respect his wishes and in the weeks that followed, legal papers were drawn up and signed. When Leo came to know a few months later (and how he learned, we don't know), the ungenial mood at home sank to new depths. For one, mandatory family dinners went from fraught to unbearable. By then, Eleonora's mother had moved into their home, albeit into a guest room on the fifth floor, where each apartment was allotted space for house guests. Confined to a wheelchair by rheumatism, Oma spent her days with her daughter on the ground floor until dinner when she was helped upstairs by her grandchildren, who went back down to get her wheelchair and fought over who would keep her company over dinner. The granddaughters especially loved Oma because she wasn't unhappy like their mother and was free with a sharp wit that made them laugh. Eleonora no longer knew where Leo spent the bulk of his days, but some things did not change. He remained particular about the stiff pleats in his pants and the shine on his shoes with brown pointed tips. As always, when he returned from work, he adjusted the paintings on the wall and counted the bonbons in the crystal bowl in the drawing room. After that, he adhered to a strict schedule for the many clocks in his home, winding up the same ones in the evening and others in the morning, so they all ran in concert, unlike his family where no one was in step with him.

He took everything that was precious to him—paintings, silver, clocks, antiques—and left behind his wife and children, ages nineteen, twenty-one, and twenty-three. My mother had escaped to Chicago by then, her brother to Toronto, so in actual fact, only his youngest child was at home. My mother once said he wouldn't have dared to leave if she'd been there, but for all her bravado, she knew he did what he wanted. In Chicago, my mother took her grandmother's advice and worked hard, complementing her office job with babysitting children on the weekends, so that she could also attend college, which her father refused to fund because she'd left Holland. Her grandmother encouraged her in long letters. *Be sensible,* Oma wrote. *Saving is fun, especially when you earn it yourself,* she elaborated sensibly, as if from experience. *And I don't know* Paris de ma fenetre. *Is it nice?* she wrote of Colette's collection, *Paris from My Window.*

My mother met my father in Chicago in 1954, the year before she returned home and discovered her mother in despair and her grandmother ridden with rheumatism and in the last weeks of life. Leo was nowhere to be found, so my mother joined the scramble to keep the household running and became a freelance tour guide. She helped her mother and sister care for her grandmother, which is why she was at bedside to witness her grandmother's startling prediction that her mother would soon join her in death. Eleonora, who leaned toward melancholy anyway, had settled there more firmly after her husband left. But after she buried her mother in Begraafplaats Buitenveldert, a century-old Catholic cemetery a short walk from the apartment, she grew less vigorous in every way. She spent much of the next year in her mother's Queen Anne chair, staring out of one of the six windows that faced the street, scarcely speaking or making any sound at all, her face damp with tears. My mother had planned on returning to the US to join my father, but the months stretched into a year before a booking agent finally sold her passage in 1956 on the SS *Amsterdam*. While my mother packed her trunk and prepared for the journey, Eleonora fell ill. A suspected flu settled deep in her lungs and wouldn't relent, despite hot compresses packed on her chest and herbal medicines slipped into her tea. Finally, a doctor made a house call. *You can't imagine what it felt like,* my mother wrote my father six months after he'd met her family, *to see my mother carried away in an ambulance.*

It was the beginning of a chapter of illness, the kind that knocks you off your feet and keeps you that way, first for a few days, then a month, and eventually for years as the rest of your life falls away or distills into disease. After their mother was admitted with tuberculosis to a University of Amsterdam clinic, my mother and aunt threw open all the windows, scrubbed the apartment with bleach, boiled sheets and towels, and then did it all over again, in the hopes of killing germs that might have taken hold. It didn't work. Or if it did, it was too late. A few weeks later, on her return from visiting a friend in Rotterdam, my mother's sister collapsed running from Amsterdam's Centraal station to the tram, and she spent the next eleven months bedridden at home with early-stage tuberculosis. More confined than she'd been even during the war, she wrote letters to her mother at the hospital two and a half miles away. When she recovered (because she, at least, did), she became a fixture on her mother's hospital ward, like the never-ending tulip supply on her mother's night table and the reading lamp affixed to her wall.

Eventually my mother boarded the ship to New York and married my father. They'd hoped to marry in North Carolina, as they'd planned, but they could not secure a marriage license because anti-miscegenation laws disallowed their marriage. They were married in Washington DC's new mosque on Massachusetts Avenue NW, the first couple to marry there. And after she whiled away much of her sick pregnancy in Lahore on a charpai on the lawn of 5 Queen's Road, she returned to Amsterdam to give birth and care for her dying mother all over again. Eleonora was not yet fifty when she died ostensibly of tuberculosis and lupus, although the truth is that heartbreak killed her.

In the final plastic sleeve in the binder of my parents' letters, I stumble upon the original *Extract from the Register of Marriage Consents*. It lists my mother's full name in bold print, *Thera Johanna Maria*. It had accompanied my mother from Amsterdam to Washington, DC, where she married my father. I think of how the *Extract* was thrown around the world. She carried it when she and my father moved to Lahore, then to Vienna where she raised young children. She carried it to Pakistan again, this time to Islamabad, where her children left home and then, finally, back to Vienna where she finished her life. It's a half-slip of middling paper, impressive only for the clarity of a minimalist red stamp in the upper right corner. I imagined it wedged in my mother's purse while she walked to the copy store on Nußdorfer Straße, where Ayesha and I would make copies of her death certificate after her death. There, she scanned a fifty-five-year-old document begrudgingly signed by a man in Amsterdam who'd disowned his children, never guessing a granddaughter in New York might one day make use of it.

Along with the *Extract*, I find Eleonora's letters (there are only three), and until I find them, she doesn't speak. I read the letter written in English and addressed to my father. Her voice is immediately familiar and oddly comforting, even though the subject matter is difficult and I require the full four pages to comprehend who is writing. Eleonora's voice is strong and clear, like my mother's, and well-suited to the *What are your intentions?* purpose. By the time she writes, Eleonora has lost her mother to death and her husband to a mistress but is still a few months away from losing her health to tuberculosis. She has met my father only twice, on his way to and back from Lahore, but she writes as if she already knows everything she needs to know about him, and perhaps she does. Eleonora sympathizes with his parents who, she says, my father must have hurt deeply with his hope to marry a Western girl, and believes his parents will need time to make peace with his choice. She appreciates my parents' love for each other, but warns the greater sacrifice will be asked of my mother. *Love can bridge over many things, but only to a certain extent,* she writes without imagining 5 Queen's Road at the other side of that bridge. She opposes her daughter returning to the US unless my father has made clear their *vast and future plans* of which, she writes, *as Thera's mother, I do not only wish, but I command to be informed. If none exist,* she says, alluding to plans for marriage, which she's not convinced my father has in mind, *I oppose her return, a hundred times.*

I sink into Eleonora's words as if they are another world and all I know. My mother's voice echoes backwards into the past, and like a conjurer's trick, both she and Eleonora come to life. The women are in conversation in my presence, but all I hear are phrases we have in common. *To a certain extent,* my mother says to clarify. *Under no circumstances,* my grandmother says, because there's something non-negotiable between them. *I command you to do as I say,* she says to my mother, just as my exasperated mother instructed me a hundred times when I refused her. Finally my mother insists, *a hundred times,* her exclamation point on all manner of sentences when nothing else would do. I hear only fragments and broken cadence. This, too, is familiar and comforting as I try to stitch together the bits and pieces (and letters) of their lives, in my quest to make them, and me, whole.

Documents are the register of my mother's life. Dates and cities fold into themselves in different forms and languages, creating a private topography of a life—birth, school, marriage, babies, death. Photographs fill out the relief: Thera at seventeen in a checked ski parka on a Swiss mountain, at thirty-eight in big sunglasses shielding her from the glare on our upstairs verandah the summer we moved to Islamabad, her grandparents' Maastricht living room years before she was born and it was bombed. In recordings, my mother and her sister lay bare more details than I can absorb, so I listen to Omar's tapes over and over again until I know before my mother and aunt know that the tenor of their voices will shift, and I know which shade of accent will roll from whom, how long they will pause while they weave their tales, and of course, the nitty gritty they will include in the sum of their lives. My aunt attended twelve different schools, my grandfather's mistress tap danced, my grandmother's sores were like purple confetti the day my mother brought her newborn to the hospital to meet her.

The only thing left to go through is a sheaf of papers in a battered pink folder held together with a ribbon and marked, *To be thrown upon my death.* I know what the letter is before I touch it. It's still in the envelope, which is how I saw it last in my mother's hands at our kitchen table. I open it and, this time, my palm smooths the letter. For the moment, it's the only document in the folder that I study and it is the only one I translate. I do not know what it means, to be disowned by your father or to make a life without him, to lose him in life and then again in death, in a letter written in a language, Dutch, I do not understand.

My parents' letters, though—they collapse time. They bring the then into now, pulling my parents as we never knew them into the present, muddying the people we knew with the ones they were before they had us, their hopes for each other and themselves forever suspended and alive. I don't know what to do with this inheritance that I do not have a word for except to say that as I have received her documents, I have received her world. Her map is mine, even as I make my own.

NINE

Endings need beginnings and my mother's death was her ending, but her beginning was less precise. I knew it in the large brush-strokes of her telling: war, paintings, heartbreak, illness. As a child, I'd heard it elsewhere, too, in the delicate chime of her mother's antique clock that rang twice an hour and required being wound every third day with a special key—which we failed to do when she was too ill to do it herself, and time had, in fact, run out. I touched it each Thanksgiving in the weave of her grandmother's formal table linens when my great-grandparents' embroidered initials flowed together and fell off the corner of my table. But my mother's ending (like my father's) had set my world adrift and I thought finding her beginning might steady it. I searched for it without knowing what I was looking for, in a binder of letters, in a shoebox of cassette recordings, in leather photo albums and washed-out captions. While I found details I could hold in my hands and turn over in my mind, they were not enough. I needed her places, the open flat country of Holland that had been hers long ago, and to see for myself how far away from Islamabad Amsterdam and Maastricht really are.

In the last months of my mother's life, I asked her to teach me what she'd learned so near the end.

"Live forward, not backward, darling," she advised without hesitation.

But backward, it seemed, is what I needed, so Naeem and I went to the Netherlands.

•

On our trip two years after her death, I bring with me a folder of items I can't do without. They include photocopies of my mother's birth announcement, an aerogramme Eleonora wrote from the hospital where she is convalescing, a map of a cemetery, my mother's passport. Other items are originals, like the photographs. The first is of Leo's family seal, on the back of which my mother writes, *Family Weapon*, and I don't know why there is such a seal nor, in retrospect, why I take it with me. I know the other photographs as intimately as if I've lived inside them. My favorite is of the family dinner the night before my mother leaves for Chicago. Her best friend, who we hope to meet, is at the table with her, and I envision her identifying the painting on the wall behind them, of which only the bottom third is visible.

Another photograph I bring with me is the folded one hidden behind others in a trifold silver frame that became mine. My grandmother's smile is shy as she glances sideways, away from the camera in her room in Binnengasthuis, a university hospital. She's no longer glowing, her face is gaunt and the Peter Pan collar of her bulky bathrobe is pulled tight to hide protruding collarbones. A book the heft of *A Strangeness in My Mind* lies open on her lap. Later, I find the series of five black and white photographs to which it belongs unmounted in a photo album, and I lay them out in order. It is winter and my grandmother has visitors, one of whom stands with her gloved hand wrapped around the iron foot railing of the hospital bed marked with an *8*. Her bed sits to one side of an immense window washed white by snow or daylight. Perhaps it is cold inside or perhaps her friends' visit is brief because the two women do not shed their coats or hats. In the final image, my grandmother is left alone holding an armful of tulips, her body curved just so around them, her shoulders poking out, the corner of her book barely visible. The creases in her robe are sculptural and she is crumpled inside. Her friends have left and I, too, hear the silence.

It's easy to guess why the photograph was folded so only her mother's upper body is visible. In the photograph my mother cropped for herself, the hospital bed, one in a row of others clad with the same crisp linens and withering patients, is out of sight and, if you don't know any better, it is possible to pretend that Eleonora's teeth are still white and she is sitting at a bright restaurant table wearing a cashmere cardigan and laughing with a lover just out of sight. But the image freezes more than a moment of joy near the end of my grandmother's life. It holds my mother's grief—black, white, gray—which suffused all she felt and touched and was after her mother died. I recognize the ballast. I wonder, like my mother must once have, if I should keep the photograph visible. Like her, though, I put it away until it comes with me to the Netherlands. It's in my purse when we find the hospital where my grandmother convalesced with tuberculosis. In the moment I stand there, before I pull it out, it occurs to me that I have carried Eleonora's world back to her.

Binnengasthuis is one of the places we have flown all this way to find, and we stumbled upon it with a map in Naeem's hand and the famous Rokin canal to our backs. In the year my grandmother spent there, I wonder if she ever contemplated an earlier name, which it never fully outgrew: Second Surgery Clinic and Former Convent. Like many church buildings, it was converted from a nunnery into a hospital in the 1500s by Protestant authorities when the Catholics were deposed. Rebuilt in the 1800s, the building we see is deserted and especially austere. A wooden fence is wrapped around the abandoned back, ready with graffiti for the laborers who are beginning renovation. I circle a set of buildings several times in search of the courtyard, but it's blocked from view. A few skinny linden trees with thick crowns grow from the sidewalk, and while they are too young for my grandmother to have observed, I wonder if she looked out from her window at the heart-shaped leaves of other lindens those many years ago.

The photograph of my grandmother in her iron hospital bed is in my hand and I try to match the immense windows flooding light with the dark and empty ones that look down on me. Leo twice sent flowers to Eleonora, and the first time, she threw them from the window before the nurses could stop her, so I study the carefully laid brick street, picturing where they might have fallen. All the doorways are tall and arched, and the oversized double doors look heavy and imposing. I imagine my mother struggling with them a day or two after giving birth when she brings her newborn to her mother. I think that if I could just unlock the doors, any of them, and run up the freshly disinfected stairs fast enough, I would catch my grandmother in bed reading and I could tell her that the Binnengasthuis will be the new University of Amsterdam library. Squeezed beside her on the narrow bed, her book open on her sunken chest, I'd put the photograph in a hand that looks like mine and we'd giggle at the vague irony until, suddenly, she is not sick anymore.

On the way back to our hotel, Naeem and I pass Café Americain, the scene of a famous family fight to which my mother had alluded. Because of Omar's recordings, I now know about the chandeliers that hang from the high ceilings, the starched tablecloths and delicate china, waiters with aprons and accordion wallets to hold coins and receipts. I want to go inside, but I worry that doing so will alter the history that, because I've imagined it my whole life, feels sacred. I'm not ready for that, so we saunter outside, listening to trams ring bells at cars and bicyclists who do and don't get out of the way. Birds play in the fountain where spouts shaped like fish shoot water into the air. The stoop at the top of the stairs is a mosaic of miniature multi-colored tiles that spells out *welcome* (which I don't feel) but we go inside anyway. There, it is dark and bright at once. The walls that face the street stream light even though one third of the windows are stained glass and it is overcast outside. The chandeliers are not what I expect, which is hundreds of tiny crystals and bulbs. Instead, they are Art Deco, full of lines and frosted panes, and shed yellow light, as do the wall lamps illuminating paintings of *A Midsummer's Night Dream* scenes. It's late afternoon, still too early for dinner service. There are fingerprints on the water glasses and there are no tablecloths, but by chance our tea arrives in teapots on trays with logos on the cup, pot, and tray lined up and facing us with an exactitude worthy of my grandfather.

By the time my aunt confronted Leo in Café Americain, her mother only had a few months to live. Leo had already attempted (without success) to have Eleonora declared mentally unfit so that he could access her money, and Eleonora, accepting defeat, had already given him a divorce. All the harm he'd done was in the past, except for the tuberculosis thriving in her lungs and a new illness, lupus, ravaging her tissues and organs. Bedridden for almost a year, my aunt had spent her time nursing anger at her father for his trespasses which later, in the presence of her mother's suffering, deepened into fury. But when her brother returned from Canada and she thought he went to see his father first, not his mother, she'd had enough.

She waited to surprise them until the appetizers were cleared and dinner was served. Leo was at home in a world of formal place settings, having mastered the act of laying a table so that each piece of silverware lay equidistant to the next. The table was covered with dishes: mixed salad, roasted potatoes, blood-streaked beef, gravy with its own silver spoon wedged in the long lip of the gravy boat, and a crystal goblet of wine sitting directly above the knives. Leo wore an expensive suit, his tie crisply knotted in his collar.

"Why haven't you visited Mams?" she asked her brother.

Then she turned to her father who sat stiff and proper at the table. He narrowed his eyes into beads, as he'd done whenever reprimanding her as a child, which she was no longer. She'd come with a litany of grievances, but in the end, they boiled into one.

"You're a beast," she said loudly enough for the closest diners to hear.

Finally, she rose. Rapt, they watched her gather the nearest ends of the starched white tablecloth into her hands as if this had been her intention all along. "You disgust me," she said to her father, and yanked the linen from the table. The china and silverware, the glass salt and pepper shakers, and the goblet, too, went flying. She waited a moment while the brown gravy and red wine dripped from her father's shirt and tie and jacket, and he absorbed the scene she'd orchestrated in the high-class establishment to which he fancied he belonged. His face reddened, his eyes blazed. When frantic waiters reached the table, she said with a hint of cheer, "I hope you enjoy your dinner." She walked between tables of dumbfounded guests, underneath Tiffany chandeliers and ceiling arches, until she reached the entrance where her friend Anna waited to drive her home. Then she quickly glanced back, just to see if her father had noticed Anna, and even from that distance she saw his face fall further and his embarrassment compound because his daughter's best friend had witnessed the scene. That, as far as anyone knew, was the last time my aunt spoke to her father.

I meet my cousin, Emile, for the first time since I was seven and he was five and we played in the sand on the North Sea and someone, perhaps his father, my mother's brother, snapped a photograph. He spends a precious day with us and drives us places we would not see otherwise—like Egmond aan Zee and its beach in the photograph. As we walk along the water, we speak of Eleonora and Leo and what could have possessed them to give up their firstborn, his father, to a grandmother, and how my mother did not recall his absence. The sea is still and there are shells, and while we walk I consider the North Sea, where our grandmother's ashes were strewn, but I forgot to ask my mother where, so now, while Emile talks, I wonder if it could have been from this beach, in the shadow of its immense lighthouse. I want to ask Emile for his version of Café Americain, but I do not. My mother had one, and it corroborated her sister's in almost every detail except her brother's presence. I expect his father, who is dead like his sisters, must have had an account as well, and Emile would know.

We have dinner at Emile's house and his mother, my aunt, joins us. I show her all my photographs and she smiles and remembers the past the way someone who has sat with it for so long; it has come back with new clarity. She does not remember the paintings, but she remembers a Greek art dealer involved in a sale. She tells stories my mother never did, like Leo's reaction to Thera's desire to marry Munir. "A Negro? That's who you want to marry?" She remembers it clearly, but I ask her anyway. "Are you sure?"

Later, in email correspondence, Emile supplies a different tale and Café Americain does not figure in it, although it has the power to sweep it all away. He tells me that when his father reached Rotterdam from Canada, he rang Eleonora to tell her he'd arrived, and she responded, two years after she'd seen him last, that ten o'clock at night was too late for him to come home and she would see him the following day. So he went to Leo's instead and there was no need for Café Americain.

Rotterdam is much colder than Egmond aan Zee. Naeem and I are there in October, the same month in 1952 that my mother sailed to Chicago for the first time. In photographs of her departure, her hair blows in the wind, as does her mother's, and they are both wearing long coats on the deck of the ship. Leo, too, stands next to his daughter. He is bundled in an overcoat and scarf, and I cannot see his hands, so I wonder if he is wearing two square rings, his favorite accoutrement, according to my aunt. During our visit, the sky roils with clouds, the light is translucent, and the brick Holland America Line terminal from which she sailed is dwarfed on either side by modern buildings. We know her ship launched from there because Emile tells me so—and he knows because he'd visited with his father who'd left for Canada from the same location. The terminal is Hotel New York now, and Naeem and I eat a large bowl of potato soup a few hundred yards from where my mother's ship would have sailed. The same wide pipes and iron staircase hang from the ceiling, and I wonder if Eleonora cried at her daughter's departure and if all their fates were already written when they stood together on the ship's deck. We take a tour of the port, where docked ships heave up and down like lumbering, breathing chests. Shipping containers are everywhere stacked like pieces of lives, one on top of each other, the messy mix of bright orange, bright blue, and red, always red, privy to a secret order. Cranes perched on docks at the water's edge appear alive, agile beings with upper and lower limbs, and for a moment, I think they may speak.

A day later, we discover Leo's office building in downtown Amsterdam at the corner of Nes and Pieter Jacobszstraat, just as it appears in a photo in my mother's final album. Leo was the sales representative for a German silver company and when he founded a subsidiary, it occupied the premises of what is now a hotel. The Art Deco building was constructed in 1904 as the largest of four theaters on the street. Others survive as theaters, but the receptionist tells us that soon after being built, Leo's building became "more of a brothel," which I try to picture as I absorb the magnificent light-filled surroundings. The glass ceiling pulls in the sky and it rests on my head as I learn the architect was Austrian and the ceiling replicates another of his buildings, the Postsparkasse in Vienna, a post office and bank where I've been.

It takes five minutes to walk from Leo's office to Binnen-gasthuis where Eleonora lay and Leo did not visit. It's farther to Minervaplein, through the flower market and museum quarters, across canals, and that's when we pass Amstel Hotel and I recall my mother linking it to her father's trespasses. It rains huge drops and we wait under an awning, where I hear tap-dancing because the detail is wrapped in my aunt's story of walking to work with her father on a Saturday morning and meeting his lover in a wide-open building that might have been a factory. I look for the building and since I don't know what I'm looking for, it is everywhere and nowhere at once.

Which is how it feels to be in Amsterdam. There are signs of my mother in everything and nothing that I see: in her school, a home now and empty of school girls; in the maternity clinic, where my mother arrived on the back of her sister's bicycle the first time she thought she was in labor, an office building now; in the Art Deco door of her apartment whose windows (and secrets) are tightly shuttered now; in her best friend who lives around the corner and serves us coffee in delicate cups on a tray the way my mother would have if she were still alive.

•

If there is a beginning, it is in Maastricht.

I have known Maastricht for as long as I can remember. The first syllable is a long exhale that has followed me my whole life. The second syllable is rushed, an exclamation point of consonants that punctuates what happened there. For all the space Maastricht inhabited in my mind, it was condensed into a single event: a bridge over the River Maas blown up by the Allies during World War II to prevent a German advance. The bombing destroyed my great-grandparents' home, and the Germans arrived anyway. As a young girl, my visiting mother was saved from the flames by jumping from the third-floor window, a leap that became a defining detail that followed her to the grave. At her funeral, Omar invoked the story, painting a life that stretched impossibly from the River Maas in one corner of the world to the Margalla Hills in another.

It's a two-hour train journey south from Amsterdam to Maastricht, which lies near the border with Belgium. The countryside speeding in my window is perfectly flat, the land an unfurled carpet. The fields seem cleaned if not polished, and rich soil is ready ahead of schedule for spring's seeds and summer's crops. A few stops outside Maastricht, Leo's village pops up in bold letters on the information screen. I'm startled to discover how deeply the name resonates with me, and just like that, my imaginings collapse into reality. *Roermond* exists outside of my mother's history; it is locatable, a physical space through which we're rushing. The village of lore and memory is fact.

On arrival in Maastricht, the town is ancient as expected but there is more than one bridge—there are seven, to be precise. Sint Servaasbrug is my mother's bridge because it is within a few yards of her grandparents' home and, like magic, the cobblestone road from the train station to our hotel leads directly to the seven-hundred-year-old bridge first built by the Romans. The bridge extends over the River Maas in a sea of bicyclists and pedestrians, and we pause at the halfway point to face the Oeverwal, a stretch of road that runs along the river. I identify my great-grandparents' home or a rebuilt version of it in all its whitewashed splendor, as if nothing, least of all war, had ever touched it. It sits on a corner, the roof steeply slanted over three stories. My great-grandfather housed his attorney office on the ground floor. Now a garage, the space once held enormous desks and wall-lined bookcases, brocaded curtains and an oriental carpet, all painstakingly preserved in a still life series of the home in Eleonora's photo albums.

Meeting memory, or coming face to face with a scrap of someone else's, changes it, and I discover other versions of my mother's wartime story. My mother jumped from the window of her grandparents' home at the end of the war, not the beginning, the bombed bridge was Wilhemina, not Sint Servaas, and it was the Germans who bombed it as they left, not the Allies who liberated Maastricht a day later on September 14, 1944. When I return to New York, I research further and discover a third possibility, that Sint Servaasbrug was bombed not once, but twice, and at both ends of the war, once by the Allies and once by the Germans. But what doesn't change is that I've mistaken my mother's age the day she hurled herself out of the window, as if World War II was so large and she so small, her age was beside the point. She is not the three- or four-year-old I've imagined; she is either five or eleven, depending on whether it's the beginning or the end of the war. My research cannot explain her decision to jump or why, in the process, she didn't break her back or limbs, or how she survived at all. In his eulogy at her funeral, Omar said our mother was caught by firemen who broke her fall. I search for them, those men with strong arms and wide nets, in war-time photographs of the Oeverwal and Sint Servaasbrug, as if I would know them.

In the final stanza of the wedding poem, *Fragments from the Diary of a Bachelor,* Leo's brother asks the newly married couple to call their home LEONORA, because the name speaks to their everlasting love and *tells it all.* The couple are forever bound, but not because of clever wordplay or marriage. Eleonora and Leo remain fixed in embrace, woven together, and in death at least she cannot do without him. Whether she is wronged, loved, or missed, there he is, always on the horizon for stealing her love and life. Which is how Eleonora has been passed on to us. In his shadow, as though without him she has no shape.

Eleonora and Leo married in a Jesuit church that (like Eleonora) had abandoned religion. In 1930, when she was not yet twenty-one, the Baroque building had already been repurposed as a theater and event venue for at least two hundred years. They married in the Redoutezaal, a room of windows and mirrors, and chandeliers whose reflections danced with the wedding guests. But there are no wedding photographs, not in my grandmother's photo albums nor in the haphazard one my mother compiled for us at the end of her life. The absence of a wedding album is suspicious, so I see Eleonora crouching near her hortensias and setting it on fire in the Minervaplein courtyard a few steps from her daughters' bedroom.

The Bonbonniere, as it was called even then, is stark and solemn from the west. It's a mysterious rectangular tower that is more fort than anything, with windows covered by brick facade. I stumble into the building from the east, through a clean and joyful entryway sporting a colorful poster of an upcoming dance festival and, curiously, a bronze plaque for the Russian consulate general's office. Inside, no one monitors the foyer, so I open the splendid doors on the ground floor and find the Redoutezaal which remains magnificent, and pale green. Tables and chairs are stacked on the sides, in case anyone needs the floor to dance, which we don't because just then the concierge finds us and wonders what we are doing in his building. He is unimpressed when I tell him about my grandparents' marriage almost a century earlier, and we are asked to leave. It doesn't change anything, because when we leave, I take the Bonbonniere, as I take all I have seen, with me.

•

Back in Amsterdam, we take the bus to my mother's old neighborhood near Beethovenstraat. We have a room in the same hotel that she stayed in with our sons a few months before she received a diagnosis that was not yet leukemia. At that time (and as was her habit), she walked faster and had more energy than anyone, even though her bone marrow had begun to fail. When we reach Beethovenstraat and climb the steep stairs to our hotel room, I wonder if she, too, had had to catch her breath. I thought of how happy it would have made her to see Naeem so well—and climb the stairs with ease. After we drop off our luggage, the first thing we do is walk a few blocks south over the Amstel canal to search for a long-ago apartment Leo and his mistress owned.

When we find the building, it strikes me as post-war and plain, unremarkable, like an affair.

My mother's work as a some-time tour guide had prepared her to take her grandchildren on exhaustive excursions of Amsterdam during their visit with her. The apartment did not feature in them, although Amstel Hotel, where her father conducted his affair, did. I know because the children documented their stay with cameras, and the next (and last) time my mother visited me in New York, she'd patiently identified each photograph while I typed in captions. Arriving at the cemetery photographs, she recounted the early morning toward the end of their Amsterdam stay when she whispered to the half-asleep children that she'd return in an hour. Not wishing to miss anything, the boys rolled out of bed and joined her on a vigil to her grandmother's grave. A year later, and with one course of chemotherapy behind her, we peered down at the photo of her grandmother's headstone and she laughed with delight at the boys beside it.

Begraafplaats Buitenveldert is a Catholic cemetery a mile from the Minervaplein apartment where my widowed great-grandmother spent the last years of her life. It's where she would have wanted to lie next to her husband, had he only been a believer. Instead, no one remembers where his ashes were scattered and she was laid to rest next to strangers, just like my mother would be, hundreds of miles southeast, in another country. It's early on a Saturday morning and there are no other visitors when Naeem and I begin our search for the grave. I swipe through our sons' photographs hoping to duplicate their route, but I'm quickly lost in a maze of paths among hundreds, maybe thousands, of graves. I scan the area for a three-figure statue visible in the photographs that stands watch over someone else's dead. I try to make sense of a deeply creased map salvaged from my mother's papers. It's oblong (like the cemetery) and covered in geometric squiggles, and it takes me more time than it should to realize that a scribbled number identifies a grave. We've walked the same rows several times when Naeem, who always knows north from south and east from west and how to rotate a map to orient us, finds it. Except my great-grandmother is no longer there. Someone else is settled into the ground, dropped there in December of the year my mother died.

I sit at the foot of grave 461. It's adorned with pots of red begonias in different states of bloom. If it still belonged to my great-grandmother, and I could plunge my arm into the earth, I'd be within reach of the twenty-six bones of her arthritic feet vanished into dust during sixty-three years of residence. Instead, I scratch at the narrow gaps in the brick path until my fingertips are tender. I smell the sweet dirt and dew mingled with the abundance of trees and bushes that aren't blooming, but might as well be given the majesty they assume. All around me, autumn is arriving. Broken sunlight spills through chestnut trees and onto my notebook. I lift my head to catch more, but it's impossible to know whether I'm warmed by the sun or gold leaves raining color on me. I'm not prepared to leave Begraafplaats Buitenveldert behind. I fiddle with my phone until I find what I need and balance it on my knee. My ears buzz, but I hear a car sputter in the distance and birds chirp in the canopy. I take a soundscape, hoping a hint of my great-grandmother, my grandmother, and my mother can be captured in a recording. As if a grief that old and full might still shiver the air.

"You children," I hear my mother say.

"Your children," I correct her.

TEN

One day, the cousin I've just come to know in Holland sends me a black and white photograph. It's the 1950s when his father photographs the inside of our grandfather's home. In the photograph, a bay window as enormous as any I've seen looks out on bare and frozen trees during a perpetual snowstorm. A wind howls and snow drifts, but I'm focused on a large painting in the middle of the frame. It hangs on the wall in the home my grandfather makes with his mistress in Laren, twenty miles southeast of his wife in Amsterdam. The photograph settles in my hands more easily than in my mind. I study the painting like I do everything, looking for her, my mother, who has been gone three years, two months, and twelve days.

It doesn't matter that it is a landscape painted more than three hundred years ago. A shepherd leans on his staff and gazes at his herd. The evening is full with sky and clouds making each other. A stunted hill sits to one side, gentle, like sculpted earth. My childhood in the shadow of the Margalla Hills has taught me that the rise is made large by perspective and the flat, flat landscape all around. One person, perhaps two, saunters in the distance where the shepherd glances and I wonder how often they meet.

I tell Omar about the photograph. He sends me a recording he made at the end of my mother's life, of a conversation I've already forgotten. She recounts the happiest day of her childhood, which is the end of World War II and her family's trip to Huize Raar, a relative's farm with fruit trees in the south of the Netherlands. She fast forwards a decade and repeats what she has maintained all along. Her father took everything of value with him when he left her mother and his children, including paintings. I listen to myself ask, *Which ones?* and I hear her shallow breaths and scratchy throat as the hospital's bedsheets slip beneath her. "Jan Steen, for example. Aelbert Cuyp." The names are familiar, like her claim, as if she has mentioned them before. When she says "Vermeer," I stop listening, as I'm certain I did then. I don't believe her because, as is her habit, she makes bold what is not and exaggerates, even near death.

The remnants of my mother's life—a painting and death announcement, letters and recordings, places and photo albums—run into each other like clouds and sky, and I do not know where one begins and the other ends. A few days later, I remember the battered pink folder and the documents I left unread as if my attention had been finite and a single notarized letter had needed it all. I untie the crushed ribbon, pass over the letter, and leaf through to the end of the folder's contents. I can't be sure of what I've found until I copy text into an online translation tool. It's my grandfather's last will and testament. The will is brief, but I sit with it for a while, aware for the first time that his second wife had a name and it is not *mistress,* not in Dutch nor in English. The document has an addendum, but it takes me another month to read because I cannot move beyond details in the will. Among the possessions he has left behind are eight kilograms fine gold, with the value, 76,880 guilders, recorded beside it. The fact, the weight, preoccupies me. I convert kilos into pounds and remember that my youngest son weighed seventeen pounds at seventeen weeks. I stack several cans of tomatoes and two two-pound weights on the kitchen counter to replicate such heft. I imagine gold bars, if that's how his gold is fashioned. Their cold and shine. His fingerprints. When I focus on the addendum, I am aware that it is an inventory before I pay to have it translated or I identify the line in the will that references it. The three-page inventory catalogs items my grandfather has sold to an art collector who will take possession of them upon his death.

I recognize the names of painters before I understand that paintings top the list. There's no Vermeer, but Aelbert Cuyp's *Herder met Schapen* is first. Jan Steen's *De Drinker* is a close second, followed by Adriaen Brouwer's *een van de vijf zintuigen*. The inventory is written in longhand (my grandfather's, although I don't know it yet), but because I know little about him, his line-by-line belongings strike me as deeply intimate. 1 burr walnut ladies' desk. 1 oval tea foot warmer. 1 blue Chinese flowerpot. 1 turtle watch. 1 familie verte serving dish with bird décor. 2 bronze women's figure candle holders. The art collector's signature appears below the date, Amsterdam, 1973, as do those of my grandfather and his new wife, who run their names together, as if to establish mass in the face of all the possessions they've given up.

I am twenty years too late to meet the art collector, who is of Greek descent and a fur trader in Utrecht, but now is also dead. I almost give up my search for a relative when I reach his daughter. She has a memory of one painting, *een van de vijf zintuigen*, which appears in another of my uncle's photographs and has spent Christmas dinners with my grandfather and the mistress who became his second wife. Before long, the daughter sends me images of both. The painting is a match, but her image of the painting is twice removed; it's a picture she takes of a picture she found in a box and she does not know what happened to the painting. My grandfather's second wife wears her hair wound into a bun like a gray hat perched on her head. She is also perched, on an armchair, slightly tilted and certainly old, as if she could easily die on a Monday two years after the Christmas dinner, as she does. I share my grandfather's inventory with the art collector's daughter. She owns the blue Chinese flowerpot and I compare her image to the blue Chinese vase I inherited from my mother, who inherited it from her grandmother, but hers depicts people, mine dragons, and they are not a set.

The photograph of the painting, the one Emile sent to me, remains on my desk. Every so often, I tuck it away with interview notes and photographs, but I'm lost without it in my sight, so it never stays away for long. I believe in this painting; it will make everything known. So I chase it single-mindedly, from museum to auction house, from one archivist to the next, until I'm advised that only (and only possibly) a catalogue raisonne can save me from a dead end. Such catalogues record a painter's oeuvre, like those of the seventeenth century and the Dutch Golden Age where Aelbert Cuyp, Jan Steen, and Adriaen Brouwer reside. I read the only relevant catalogue raisonne I can access online, a translation of Hofstede de Groot's outdated work of Dutch painters with few reproductions. It takes me days as I linger over descriptions of each Aelbert Cuyp painting, my heart quickening each time I read *shepherd* or *sheep*, until I contemplate an entry which mentions neither. And just like that, *Item #141* transforms my faulty black and white reproduction. It's morning, not afternoon in the painting, the hill is not a hill but is a hovel and, beside the hovel, is a man on an ass, who might sleep there. Most significant is the rambling title, *A view of the open flat Country in Holland, exhibited under the aspect of a fine summer's morning.* Armed with it, I locate the painting in a digital archive, and in a quick moment it saturates my screen.

Colors wash over me, as they do the *flat Country in Holland.* The sky is a wave of golden purple three hundred years after paints made this sky that is more alive than mine. Slanted light ripples the scene. A glorious yellow ochre holds the middle of the painting the way the middle holds me. I count more than a dozen sheep resting quietly on land too meager to cough up more than stones rounded by centuries of waiting. Far away, a church spire rises behind a river. The horizon lifts the sky and unfolds a liminal space, like the space opening in me. It's sunset here and sunrise there, and I have room for both.

I begin to write.

•

Before the pandemic, Naeem and I and our children are in Pakistan to visit family. We travel to Islamabad before spending the holidays with Ayesha and her family in Karachi.

The haunted house of my Islamabad childhood, that remnant of the 1971 war, has vanished. I do not know where the house and its ghosts or the squatters and their laundry have gone. I cannot find its replacement, which lies hidden in plain sight in a row of homes I don't remember seeing before. My parents are gone, as are their houses. Our childhood home, at which yellow school buses stopped, was razed to the ground where it stayed for years before it was replaced by two identical houses, each with a red roof, as if the blue sky and green hills were not sufficiently colorful for the owners. My parents' house, an unfinished shell in my first memory of Islamabad when my father lines us up to take a photograph and a different sort of shell after he dies, is now recognizable only by its gate and the coincidence of the owner's name that is also my father's name.

From the sidewalk, where my sons and I stand, the windows of Noor's room are visible, but like all of them, they are newly cloaked in iron grates. The spacious lawn where Ayesha married and our children played cricket is supplanted by a building, a windowless annex in need of a coat of paint. But it's still home, in a way, so we take pictures of the jumble until the chowkidar who is watching from a chair walks up to stop us. The guard isn't reassured when I explain it had been my parents' home and, as evidence, wave in the direction of their bedroom as if they might appear. He allows me one last photograph (of him) before he pulls the heavy gate closed. The low rumble of the gate's wheels on rails prevents me from leaving. It is lifted whole from my memory, a sound I would have known anywhere, despite the nineteen years since I'd last drawn closed the gate. I stand perfectly still, wanting to hear it again, hear it being exactly as it was.

"Come," one of my sons says, and leads me away.

I want to share the coincidence of the owner's name, M. Khan, with my mother and the gall of the chowkidar with my father. When we return to Ithaca, I open the diary my father kept when he was young, the one my mother only gave me when she was old. I read as if I knew him then and his words are meant for me. *And the moon grows old with us,* my father, Munir, writes in all caps (and hyperbole) the summer after Partition, when he was in his twenties and desperate for a world beyond 5 Queen's Road. *I want to explore all the corners of my life,* he writes in one of his last entries, and I wonder what he would have made of my pilgrimage, with his grandchildren, to the remains of our Islamabad home. A small photograph of Murree falls from a page on which he is angry at his father for not granting permission to travel to the hill station beyond Islamabad, to which he took us often. Now that I'm looking for the corners of my life, I imagine asking my father about his. Where do they begin and end? I wonder if he thought of himself as his father's or his mother's child. As though we belong to only one parent and the border between them is fixed, even loosely, like the borders of Pakistan or 5 Queen's Road, which have moved, like the passage of time, without regard to us.

Before Ayesha and I look at the photocopies of all my parents' letters that I have brought for her to Karachi, we compare my mother's three attempts at writing her life story. She found one on my mother's computer and I found the others buried in her papers. Each is a decade apart and the oldest, written soon after

Naeem and I married, is folded in eighths and composed on her Remington typewriter. The Remington was a going away gift from her mother, the same machine she used to write weekly letters to her children when we left home, and it is almost identical to her brother's, which Naeem was first to notice displayed in Emile's home. In that version, my mother's life story begins, *I was born out of two parents who were as different as day and night.*

"She's right," Ayesha says. "We are born out of our parents and their parents' parents."

The next day, I try to convince my family to join me on one last outing. Naeem prefers to read a biography of Freud in the sun, and Kamal and Shahid, young men now, have exhausted their leave from jobs. Alone, I visit Chowkandi, an ancient city of the dead, and at first glance it is all pale pink sandstone and dust. An hour outside of Karachi, smog hangs in the vast sky above the graveyard made hundreds of years ago. The two-mile necropolis is starved for moisture; spare and stunted brush is ash white, as if it burned rather than grew into existence. The tombs are towers of rectangles that decrease in size, pyramid-like, as they rise, often taller than me, sometimes with live eagles perched on top. There are no gravestones as we know them, and few names, but the intricate carvings that cover the sarcophagi spill other details—male or female, married or not, adult or child. Human remains lie below ground from which empty sepulchers rise like they contain great riches, not just secrets. The place is desolate with grief and beauty, holding both with equal sway.

I step around a baby's tomb and reach a cluster of adults that rises in uneven heights. The only other visitors, a young couple picnicking with a child, are elsewhere, so I do what I want. I rub my hands up and down the ancient sandstone as if I'm massaging a human being back to life. I take my time. The sandstone tickles and I taste the chalky dust in my mouth. Here, within sight and reach of other-worldly tombs, it's possible to hold on to the dead, my dead, a bit longer.

We leave Chowkandi through an adjacent lot where Pakistan's famously decorated trucks litter the landscape in all manner of disrepair. So soon after traveling to her city, I see what my mother must have seen: nothing could be farther from *the open flat Country in Holland* than Pakistan. Cabs are unhinged and bowed, windows are lost, and Nissan truck frames stand naked, recently shed. Amidst the clutter, the air conditioning sucks a waft of baking bread into the car. In between the trucks are canals of garbage dotted with the country's signature blue plastic bags, and here and there, men work, children play, and women are nowhere to be seen. The return drive is filled with the cacophony of a mega-city that doesn't extend that far, even as the roar suggests otherwise. Trucks, buses, cars, vans, rickshaws, motorcycles, bicyclists, donkey carts, pedestrians—every possible mode of transportation is well represented.

But I'm focused on sightings of *Maersk* and *Hamburg Süd* shipping containers. They are in truck beds and on roadsides and, once in a while, walled-off and piled sky-high like gray and red Lego pieces. It's not the first time I've noticed them in Karachi, a port city like Rotterdam where I photographed them last, but they hold my attention. When Thera first arrived by ship in Karachi in 1958, it was already summer in the then-capital and lack of rain was only the beginning of what she would need to make peace with. Owning little, and uncertain how long they'd stay, my parents' newly married lives slipped into a suitcase, maybe two. When we pass a bright and shiny *Hamburg Süd,* I think it could make a home. The *Maersk* is Danish, but it is also plain, a gargantuan empty coffin. *Triton, Seaco, Tex, P&O Nedlloyd, Beacon, DCG, Cronos*—all are mysteries whose origins I don't know, but their convergence in Karachi is fleeting. They will be thrown across the world again, some to Rotterdam where my mother's leaving began.

That is not exactly in the neighborhood we saw on the map, my great-grandmother writes in Amsterdam when my mother, still single, considers moving from Chicago to New Orleans.

I wonder what she might have said of Pakistan. And us.

The End

ACKNOWLEDGMENTS

Excerpts of chapters were published in various forms. I am grateful to those publications and to my editors for their faith and support. Thank you to Hillary Brenhouse and *Guernica* ("5 Queen's Road"), Sari Botton and *Longreads* ("Raising Brown Boys in Post-9/11 America"), Mehvash Amin and Ilona Yusuf and *The Aleph Review* ("Cities in Me"), and Elizabeth Dauphinee and the *Journal of Narrative Politics* ("The Silence and Forgetting That Wrote NOOR").

I am indebted to many people for generous assistance in the research for this book, including Diteke de Ruijter-Ekema and RKD—Netherlands Institute for Art History (The Hague), Kassiani Kagouridi and the Museum of Asian Art (Corfu), David Peter Coppen and the Sibley Music Library at the Eastman School of Music (Rochester), Dr. Gudrun Swoboda and the Kunsthistorisches Museum (Vienna), Samantha Chao and the Asia Art Archive (Hong Kong), Caroline Wittop Koning and Camilla Verweel and the Rijksmuseum (Amsterdam), Julia Philippens and Guusje van den Boorn-Baltis and the Regionaal Historisch Centrum Limburg (Maastricht), Giota Pavlidou and the Constantinos A. Doxiadis Archives (Athens), Amin Gulgee, Emile Eijck, Diana Chiotakis, Amanullah De Sondy, Augustinos Touloupis, Mehreen Saeed, Javed Akhtar, Liesbeth Dirks-Jessen, Martijna Briggs, Waltraud Torossian, Brigitte Neubacher, and Wies van Leuken.

Thank you to close friends and fellow writers who read versions of this work, including Laura McNeal, Joel Dinerstein, Lily King, Lisa Loomis, Patricia Dutt, Sehba Sarwar, Patricia Zimmermann, Jane Marie Law, Aida Hozić, and Douglas Unger. Thank you also to Kamini Ramani, Dawn Douglas-Coker, Denise Stover, Cindi Tashman, Lori Leonard, Rebecca Thompson, and Zillah Eisenstein.

My thanks to my exceptional editor, Kristen Elias Rowley, for her immediate and continuous enthusiasm. Thank you also to Samara Rafert, Tara Cyphers, and the wonderful team at Mad Creek Books and The Ohio State University Press.

The deepest gratitude and love is for my family. To my parents, Thera and Munir Khan, whose love for us continues to inspire and whose worlds I cannot do without. To my siblings, Omar and Ayesha, without whom I cannot imagine my journey. As ever (and always), to Naeem and to Kamal and Shahid, who make everything possible.

MACHETE
Joy Castro, Series Editor

This series showcases fresh stories, innovative forms, and books that break new aesthetic ground in nonfiction—memoir, personal and lyric essay, literary journalism, cultural meditations, short shorts, hybrid essays, graphic pieces, and more—from authors whose writing has historically been marginalized, ignored, and passed over. The series is explicitly interested in not only ethnic and racial diversity, but also gender and sexual diversity, neurodiversity, physical diversity, religious diversity, cultural diversity, and diversity in all of its manifestations. The machete enables path-clearing; it hacks new trails and carves out new directions. The Machete series celebrates and shepherds unique new voices into publication, providing a platform for writers whose work intervenes in dangerous ways.